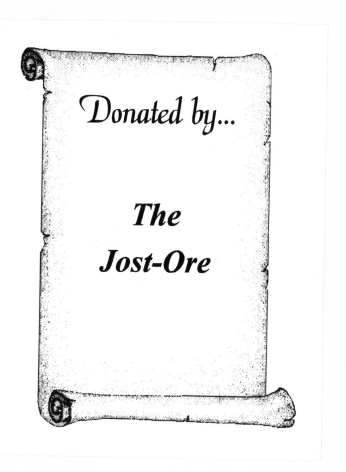

THE
INDUSTRIALIZATION
OF EUROPE:
1780–1914

1 Tools of modern industry proudly
displayed on the membership
certificate of the United Machine
Workers' Association, England, 1844

THE INDUSTRIALIZATION OF EUROPE: 1780–1914

W. O. HENDERSON

with 141 illustrations, 18 in colour

THAMES AND HUDSON · LONDON

To my grand-daughters Frances and Joanna

PRINTED IN GREAT BRITAIN BY JARROLD AND SONS LTD, NORWICH

500 32013 6 CLOTHBOUND
500 33013 1 PAPERBOUND

CONTENTS

I INDUSTRIAL GROWTH

2 The Prince Consort's ticket
to the Great Exhibition of 1851

When the Chinese reformer Huang Tsun-hsien visited London in the 1890s he found it hard to believe that, only a century before, the economy of his homeland and that of Britain had basically resembled each other. He saw Britain with her teeming industries, while the China he had recently left was still a land of village crafts and paddy-fields. In the eighteenth century the economies of all nations had been predominantly agrarian. At that time the great economic and social transformation which was to gain Europe ascendancy in world affairs had not yet taken place. But by 1890 the industrialization of the greater part of the continent was virtually complete. European power had become unchallengeable and the territories of Asia, Africa and the Pacific were falling to the empire-builders.

It was one of the major transformations in history: in no more than a hundred years a Europe of country estates, peasant holdings and domestic workshops became a Europe of sprawling industrial cities. Hand tools and simple mechanical contrivances were replaced by machines, the craftsman's cottage by the factory; steam and electricity supplanted the traditional energy sources – water, wind and muscle. Country folk, their former occupations redundant, migrated to the mining and manufacturing towns to become the workers of the new age, while a professional class of entrepreneurs, financiers and managers, of scientists, inventors and engineers, sprang into prominence and expanded rapidly. This was the Industrial Revolution.

It is clear, however, that this 'revolution' was no single process. It is possible, for example, to distinguish between a

3, 4 An end and a beginning. Above, *The Fighting 'Téméraire' Towed to Her Last Berth* (1838) by J. M. W. Turner. Right, harbinger of the factory age, Richard Arkwright's cotton mill built at Cromford in 1771. Detail of a painting by Joseph Wright of Derby

'revolution of coal and iron' lasting approximately from 1780 to 1850, and a 'revolution of steel and electricity' occurring between 1850 and 1914. It is also possible to show that industrialization affected the countries of Europe at different times and speeds. While in Britain, the first country to become industrialized, the process began in the eighteenth century (in the 1780s according to some historians; others favour the 1740s), certain parts of Europe were not industrialized until very much later. For example, as recently as 1914 comparatively little progress had been made south of the Pyrenees or the Alps, other than in northern Italy. For the most part, however, the industrialization of Europe took place before 1900.

Britain had shown the way. In the second half of the eighteenth century her expanding economy began to 'take off'. In 1790 her coal output exceeded 10 million tons; a hundred years earlier the figure had been less than 3 million tons. Pig-iron production rose from 17,000 tons in 1740 to 250,000 tons in 1806. Raw-cotton imports soared from about 1 million lb in 1743 to over 60 million lb in 1802. By the early 1820s cotton manufactures amounted to no less than 46 per cent of Britain's total exports and at the time of the Great Exhibition of 1851 Britain's cotton industry was equal in size to all other European cotton industries combined. By 1800 various regions were already specializing in the manufacture of particular products. Cotton yarn and piece-goods were made in Lancashire, woollens in the West Riding, hosiery in Nottinghamshire, steel and cutlery in Sheffield, iron and steel in southern Wales, metal goods and hardware in Birmingham and the Black Country and pottery in Staffordshire. Already Britain was indisputably 'the workshop of the world'.

In contrast, Germany, France and Italy were still agrarian countries in 1815. In Germany the production of manufactured goods was mainly in the hands of craftsmen, while modern

5, 6 The Black Country. Victorian impressions of Britain's industrial heartland. Below, the spread of industry seen as a forest fire rampaging over the Wolverhampton countryside. Right, a more literal view: factories at Leeds

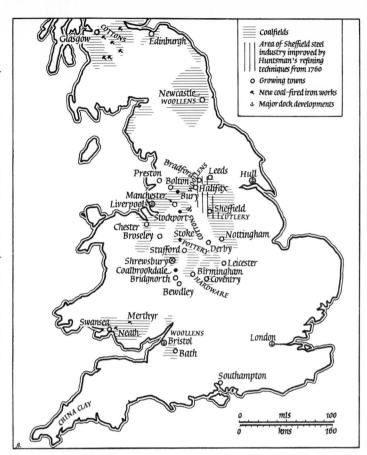

7 Map showing the advanced state of British industry in 1815—a year often taken to mark the beginning of the Industrial Revolution on the Continent. The presence of areas rich in both coal and iron and readily accessible to water transport partly explains Britain's lead. Notice the concentration of manufacturing industries in these areas; notice, too, urban growth as workers are drawn to the mining and factory towns

Coalfields

Area of Sheffield steel industry improved by Huntsman's refining techniques from 1760

○ Growing towns

↙ New coal-fired iron works

⚓ Major dock developments

industry was confined to a few pockets in the Rhineland, Saxony and Upper Silesia. It was not until after the formation of the German customs union (Zollverein) and the construction· of railways in the 1840s that rapid progress could be made and the Ruhr district experience its first industrial boom. And it was not until after the political unification of 1871 that the pace of German industrialization could rise to the feverish tempo it attained in the last quarter of the nineteenth century.

In France, despite the territorial and financial losses suffered after Waterloo, the Revolutionary and Napoleonic reforms survived. The abolition of feudalism, the creation of a central bank and a commercial code, the introduction of the metric system, and advances in chemical knowledge were permanent gains. But industrial growth, very slow during the period of the Restoration (1815–30), was retarded by poor communications, slender coal resources and a conservative populace. Under Louis-Philippe, however, bankers and manufacturers became a power behind the throne and the ground was prepared for the

8 German and French industry lagged far behind British in the first half of the nineteenth century. Helping to maintain Britain's early lead were machine tools such as the steam hammer invented by James Nasmyth in 1832. Nasmyth himself painted this scene at his foundry near Manchester

acceleration of industrial growth which occurred in the reign of Napoleon III (1852–70).

Italy in 1815 was, like Germany, divided into several States, a number under foreign control. Moreover, Italy lacked the resources of coal and iron-ore needed for a country to become industrialized in the nineteenth century. It was largely owing to Cavour's strenuous efforts to foster the economic expansion of the Kingdom of Sardinia, followed by the political unification of the country, that the way was paved for industrialization north of the Po.

THE GREAT INVENTIONS

Technological progress had been a powerful stimulus to the early growth of British manufactures. A succession of great inventions in the second half of the eighteenth century revolutionized the textile, metal and transport industries. Ingenious spinning, weaving and carding machines appeared; new ways of smelting and purifying iron-ore and a method of making crucible cast steel were devised. The cylinder-boring machine, the hydraulic press, the steam hammer and the slide-rule had transformed the engineering industry. So important did Mantoux consider this era of inventions that he felt justified in closing his account of the Industrial Revolution in 1800 because 'by then the great technical inventions – including the most important of all, the steam-engine – had all become practical realities'.

Britain owed much of her technical knowledge to other European countries. In the seventeenth century the mining engineers of Germany, the canal-builders of Holland and French civil engineers had led the world in their fields and Britain had frequently drawn upon their expertise. German engineers, for example, had helped to open up the Cumberland copper-mines and Dutch experts had helped to drain the Fens. In Derbyshire an Italian had set up England's first silk-throwing mill. But mainland Europe had been unable to capitalize on her initial advantage and Britain was able to turn the tables. In the

9 Ironmasters on the coalfields of Upper Silesia were among the first in Germany to adopt coke-smelting. Above, the Royal Foundry at Gleiwitz, 1841

second half of the eighteenth century John Holker took British textile machines and skilled operatives to Normandy, Michael Alcock established several metalworks in France, William Wilkinson introduced coke-smelting at the Le Creusot iron-works and Tarnowitz leadworks, while John Baildon erected coke-furnaces at two ironworks in Silesia. At the same time foreigners visited Britain to spy out the new methods and persuade skilled artisans to migrate illegally across the Channel.

After the Napoleonic Wars the industrial methods with which Englishmen had long been familiar gradually came into general use abroad. Mulhouse and Elberfeld-Barmen, though far behind Lancashire, emerged as leading cotton districts. And even in Russia, at that time hardly on the threshold of indus-trialization, modern cotton-mills were built. Mainland Europe also had its inventors. In France, for example, an improved

15

locomotive boiler and new wool-carding machines were developed, while Swiss and German metallurgists discovered how to make crucible cast steel, for long a British monopoly.

In the second half of the nineteenth century a spate of inventions on both sides of the Channel was to transform the face of industry once again. New techniques in steel-making opened the way for the economic production of high-quality steel on a vast scale; the steam turbine, the internal-combustion engine and the electric motor arrived to challenge the reciprocating steam engine; and dramatic advances in chemistry laid the foundations for the plastics and pharmaceuticals industries.

THE RAILWAY REVOLUTION

A further reason for Britain's early industrialization lies in the fact that her location on the edge of western Europe

10 Satire on the potential of steam locomotion (*c.* 1830) by the cartoonist Shortshanks

11 Impressive evidence of a breakthrough in the economics of steel-making—the Eiffel Tower, as depicted by Seurat ▶

12, 13, 14 Heavy industry can only thrive where efficient transport facilities are available. Before the coming of the steam locomotive, countries like Britain, with a highly developed coastal trade and extensive system of inland waterways, held a clear advantage. Left, shipping coal at Seaham Harbour in the early nineteenth century. Right, dawn of the railway age: the historic opening of the Stockton–Darlington line, 1825. Below, an irksome routine before the rationalization of railway gauges: transhipping goods at Gloucester, 1846

gave her immediate access to the world's important trade routes and enabled her to open up great overseas markets. Her numerous harbours enabled her to develop an active coastal trade. The widespread presence of navigable rivers helped to foster inland trade, and the fact that her coalfields were often conveniently situated near the ports made it possible for her to develop industries based on coal at a time when other countries still relied on wood for fuel and used charcoal as a smelting agent. Internal communications were further improved by the construction of a canal network, the provision of new roads by turnpike trusts, and the building of tramways to serve collieries, mines, quarries and factories. The rest of Europe had to await the age of steam before industrialization could begin in earnest.

The building of railways was probably the most important single factor in promoting European economic progress in the 1830s and 1840s. Again Britain, where the first public passenger line (from Stockton to Darlington) was opened in 1825, was the pioneer and could act as consultant and supplier abroad.

Belgium and Germany quickly appreciated the value of rail communications. Belgium lay at the crossroads of Europe and the port of Antwerp had made her a centre of world trade. She also possessed valuable coal deposits in the valleys of the Sambre and the Meuse. Upon gaining her independence in the 1830s she promptly constructed a network of State railways radiating from Brussels, thereby assuring her future as a major centre of industry and commerce.

In Germany Cologne became an important railway centre, with lines running to Antwerp, Minden and Basel. Berlin, with lines running to Hamburg, Stettin, Anhalt, Breslau, Magdeburg and Leipzig, also acquired a new significance. The coal of the Ruhr penetrated new and distant markets and the growth of Germany's North Sea ports was greatly accelerated. The demand for rails promoted the expansion of the German iron industry and, although much early equipment came from England, Belgium and even the United States, German firms, such as Borsig of Berlin, were soon supplying locally built locomotives and rolling-stock. The building of the rail network,

15 Locomotive engine: an example of engineering draughtsmanship, 1848

16 Paris railway station, *Gare Saint-Lazare*, as painted by Monet, 1877

coinciding as it did with the formation of the Zollverein, played an important part in overcoming the economic barriers which divided one German State from another.

In France the construction of railways was retarded for political reasons. For several years it remained uncertain who was to be responsible for planning and finance, and a law providing for the construction of a network of lines radiating from Paris was not passed until 1842. There was at once a boom in track-laying. Lines from Paris to Rouen and Le Havre and to Lille and Calais were among the earliest to be completed. The first (built by English contractors) linked Paris with an important textile region and major seaport, while the second brought the coalfields, ironworks and textile mills of the Nord Department closer to the capital and created a link with London and Brussels.

21

By 1870 a web of steel stretched across western Europe embracing even those countries, like Spain and Italy, which were late and slow to develop. It had become a simple operation to move heavy machinery and raw materials in great quantity from one corner of the Continent to another. Already railway engineers had pierced the Alps at Mont Cenis and the plans of the St Gotthard Tunnel were off the drawing-board.

SOCIAL ADAPTABILITY

Some countries found it much easier than others to accept the social changes involved in the transition from an agrarian to an industrial economy. A society with a well-developed middle class, flexible class divisions and workers who could learn new skills and accept a new kind of discipline, was likely to evolve more rapidly than a society burdened with a weak middle class, rigid class barriers and a highly conservative peasantry. The legacies of feudalism therefore seriously retarded early industrialization in Europe. The survival of serfdom in many countries – in France until the Revolution, and in Germany, Austria and Russia until well into the nineteenth century – made it virtually impossible to recruit a modern industrial labour

17 Mindful of Italy's slender coal resources and enthusiasm for railways, a patriotic inventor hatched the *Impulsoria* of 1853

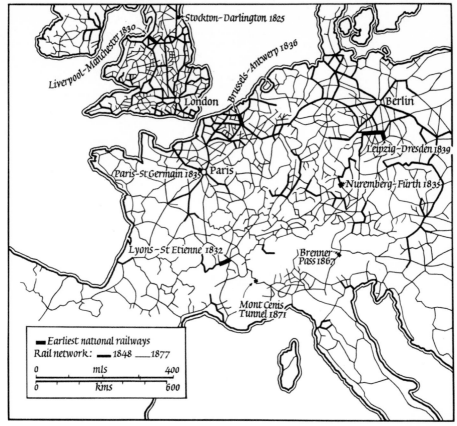

Stockton–Darlington 1825

Liverpool–Manchester 1830

Brussels–Antwerp 1836

London

Berlin

Leipzig–Dresden 1839

Paris–St Germain 1835 Paris

Nuremberg–Fürth 1835

Lyons–St Etienne 1832

Brenner
Pass 1867

Mont Cenis
Tunnel 1871

■ Earliest national railways
Rail network: ▬ 1848 ▬ 1877

0   mls   400
0   kms   600

18 Map indicating the pace of railway development in central Europe between 1848 and 1877. Industrial growth is most marked where the network is densest

force. Workers were subject to the rules and privileges of craft guilds and municipalities and generally had to obtain permission to migrate from one province to another.

In eighteenth-century Britain, however, serfdom had already vanished and the restrictions imposed by guilds and municipal authorities upon pioneer industrialists were not as severe as in many places across the Channel. Entrepreneurs had little to fear from government interference, particularly if they set up their factories outside municipal boundaries; workmen could move freely from one part of the country to another. In Britain, moreover, there were no rigid barriers between town

23

19, 20 That a spinning wheel could sprout a thousand spindles is one measure of the Industrial Revolution. Left, *The Spinster at the Hearth*— a traditional cottage scene. Below, *Mule Spinning* (1835)

21 Right, titled entrepreneur of eighteenth-century England, Francis Egerton, third Duke of Bridgewater, canal-builder and coal-magnate

and countryside. On the one hand owners of landed estates were prepared to exploit their own mineral resources and had no objection to members of their families taking an active part in commercial and manufacturing enterprises. On the other hand successful manufacturers from the towns could buy estates in the country, and their families entered the ranks of the landed gentry. There developed a middle class sufficiently large and varied to furnish many of the entrepreneurs and managers of the new factories. At the same time British peasants and crafts-men moulded well into a modern labour force. It is true that there was vociferous Luddite opposition to the new machines and the harsh discipline of the pioneer factories, but the Luddites comprised only a small minority of the workers. Industrial progress was rapid.

25

In France conditions were less favourable, and industrial progress slow. Peasant proprietors and tenant farmers were deeply attached to the land and strongly influenced by family ties, and it was difficult to attract them to the towns and factories. They were hard-working and thrifty and invested heavily in land or government bonds. They were suspicious of banks and reluctant to risk their money in railway shares or other joint-stock enterprises. In the towns the middle classes were hardly less conservative. Whether engaged in retail trade, craft-work or industry they tended to work in closely knit family units. The family firm was the traditional type of industrial organization, the large joint-stock company the exception. Moreover, a highly centralized system of government reacted on the economy. The provinces, accustomed to look to Paris for a lead, were reluctant to initiate their own economic ventures.

THE IMPACT OF WAR

War had a special influence on the development of the Industrial Revolution in Europe, working in certain sectors of the European economy as a severe depressant, in others as a powerful spur to progress. While Britain waged her wars abroad in the eighteenth and nineteenth centuries, her neighbours across the Channel were frequently disturbed by a military presence. Often the results in these countries were wholly negative. At the end of the Seven Years War, for example, Prussia's population had declined by 330,000; towns, villages, manors, farms, workshops and bleaching-grounds had been destroyed and in some districts acute shortages of food and fodder were experienced. The currency was debased, public finances were in disorder and civil administration was in danger of collapsing. In Poland the ravages of war had led to famine and plague, which together in 1770 caused a quarter of a million deaths.

It is something of a paradox therefore that twenty-three years of Revolutionary and Napoleonic Wars should subsequently have marked the beginning of industrial expansion on

22 By order of Napoleon: French soldiers burning British imports in 1810

the European mainland. Naturally Europe suffered. The movement of great armies living off the land, heavy casualties and the massive diversion of manpower from more peaceful pursuits had their inescapable consequences, while Napoleon's 'Continental System' and the British blockade ruined one great port after another. Certain industries, however, expanded enormously under wartime pressures. The need to clothe, provision and arm many thousands of soldiers created an almost insatiable demand for certain commodities – a demand greatly accentuated by the exclusion of British competition. Striking growth was evident in the cotton industries of Ghent, Paris, Mulhouse and Saxony and in the metal and armament industries of Belgium, Germany and Switzerland. Great engineering firms, such as John Cockerill's works at Liège and the Escher-Wyss plant at Zürich, came into being. Moreover, in the days when Napoleon controlled much of western and central Europe French experts were sent into less developed regions to carry out geographical surveys, prospect for minerals and supervise the operation of certain mines and factories.

27

Napoleon's Continental System had been intended, not as a stimulus to European industry, but as a war measure designed to undermine Britain's economy by curtailing her export trade. Indeed, Britain was not unscathed; by 1816 she had incurred a national debt of £876 million and there were periods of serious financial disturbance, unemployment and social distress. But already Britain's industrial progress had been such that, despite the loss of valuable markets on her doorstep, British merchants were able to maintain exports by opening up new markets in South America and elsewhere. Britain's great industries continued to expand and her capacity to dominate the high seas, support Wellington's armies in the Peninsular War and finance the war effort of her allies with substantial subsidies remained unimpaired.

The effects of war upon industrial growth were particularly marked in Russia. As Gerschenkron points out, economic development in Russia in the nineteenth century actually became 'a function of military exigencies. . . . It proceeded fast whenever military necessities were pressing and subsided as the military pressure was relaxed.' The disclosure of economic weaknesses in time of war would lead to vigorous action afterwards: the Crimean War was a spur to the emancipation of the serfs and the expansion of the railway system, while the Turkish War of 1876 was followed by a great drive to expand Russia's heavy industries.

THE PROMOTION OF INDUSTRY, 1840–70

In the period 1840–70 the encouragement of industry and agriculture by the State and the founding of credit banks and joint-stock companies were probably the most significant incentives to economic progress on the European mainland. The slump of 1847 and the Revolutions of 1848 were followed by a period of economic expansion interrupted only by the depression of 1857 and the dislocation of the cotton industry during the blockade of the Southern States at the time of the Civil War in the United States. The authoritarian régimes

THE RAILWAY MANIA   THE MOMENTOUS QUESTION.

23, 24 Left, 'What! you're at it again. Writing for railway shares!' Right, 'Tell me, oh tell me, dearest Albert, have *you* any railway shares?'

holding power in countries such as Austria, France and Prussia in the period of reaction that followed the Revolutions relied upon the support of the middle classes and passed laws favourable to the expansion of industrial and commercial activities. In Prussia, for example, the reform of the mining laws lifted numerous restrictions which had long inhibited private mining enterprise. Throughout Europe the urban middle classes, still largely unable to participate directly in the political life of their countries, devoted their energies to economic undertakings.

In the 1850s and 1860s various factors greatly extended the market for European manufactured goods. The continued growth of population, the extension of railway networks in Europe and the United States, the introduction of iron steamships, the opening of the Suez Canal, and a renewed bid for colonial possessions, all greatly benefited international trade.

25 A new trade route to the East: the Mediterranean meets the Red Sea as Ferdinand de Lesseps's Suez Canal nears completion in the summer of 1869

British authority was extended in India and the suppression of the Mutiny of 1857 was followed by a programme of capital investment which brought orders to British ironmasters and other industrialists. The French strengthened their grip on Algiers and the increase in commerce between France and her colony in North Africa was reflected in the expansion of Marseilles. Meanwhile, the Russians were pressing forward in Siberia and Central Asia.

Economic expansion was also stimulated by the reduction of tariffs in western Europe. Britain was the first country to adopt free trade: with the repeal of the Corn Laws and the budgets of Peel and Gladstone, nearly all import duties were abolished. The Anglo-French (Cobden) commercial treaty of 1860 and the Franco-Prussian (Zollverein) treaty of 1862 provided for drastic reductions in France's high import tariffs. By 1870 many countries of western Europe were linked in a low-tariff *bloc*. And the creation of the Austro-German and Latin monetary unions showed that governments were beginning to appreciate the importance of securing a fixed relationship between the major currencies.

In several countries the State exercised direct control over a nationalized sector of the economy, and at the same time offered financial assistance to private enterprise. Mines, ironworks, saltworks, naval dockyards, armament factories, railways and various other public utilities and industrial enterprises were operated as nationalized concerns. In Prussia, for example, the Saar coal-mines were nationalized.

Although nationalized concerns and private firms, such as Krupp of Essen, were of great importance, the growth of major industrial regions like the Ruhr was mainly due to the activities of joint-stock companies. Regarded with suspicion by governments and civil servants since the historic collapse of the South Sea Company in the previous century, these companies had mainly been confined to the fields of public utilities and mining. Now they became a powerful instrument of industrialization. Between 1850 and 1857 some 170 joint-stock companies were set up in Prussia alone.

Bankers and financiers now played a vital role in fostering new enterprises. In the 1850s a new kind of finance house came into prominence, the Crédit Mobilier in France, the Darmstadt Bank in Germany and the Kreditanstalt in Austria being among the most important examples. They attracted the savings of small investors and used them to buy shares in new industrial enterprises. In 1856 the French Consul in Leipzig reported that in Germany 'every town and state, however small it may be, wants its bank and its Crédit Mobilier'.

These credit banks, which soon spread to Italy, Spain, Holland and other countries, were more closely involved with industry than the older British banks. Being the first nation to industrialize, Britain, as Landes observes, 'was able to build her plant from the ground up . . . beginning with rudimentary machines that were not too expensive for private purses and ploughing profits into growth and technological advance'. In Britain joint-stock companies and credit institutions were less important than they proved to be elsewhere.

INDUSTRIAL PROGRESS, 1870–1914

The years between 1870 and 1914 witnessed a rapid increase in the pace of European industrialization and a sharp intensification of interest in new colonial markets. The older colonial Powers Britain and France extended their possessions in Africa and the Pacific. In the 1880s Germany, Italy and Belgium joined the scramble for new colonies. Bismarck secured certain African territories for Germany, although their economic value proved to be limited; Belgium acquired a colony in the Congo; and Italy had to be content with Libya and part of Somaliland.

Britain remained foremost among manufacturing nations, but others, especially Germany, were beginning to challenge her lead. The time came when Britain's pioneer role proved to have its drawbacks. Machines once the best in the world were now less efficient than newer models developed abroad and British marketing methods were outdated. In the days when Britain had virtually monopolized the sale of certain manufactures in foreign markets the customer had little option but to accept what was offered. Now, British salesmen found it difficult to adapt to a competitive situation. Moreover, many British industrialists persisted in training their labour force on traditional lines, ignoring more efficient modern methods.

Germany provided much of the impetus for the new burst of industrial activity and innovation distinguishing the last quarter of the nineteenth century. Prussia's victory at Sedan and the creation of a united Reich had greatly strengthened German morale. Although in 1873 a slump followed the post-war boom of 1871–2 rapid growth occurred not only in Germany's old-established industries, such as iron, steel, coal and textiles, but also in shipbuilding, chemicals and the electrical industry. Great cartels well suited to the conditions of the time were allowed to develop. There was striking expansion in the export of manufactured products and in invisible exports, such as banking, insurance, and shipping services. Before 1870 Germany had been a borrower on the international money-market, but thereafter her national wealth increased to such an extent that she was able to invest large sums in mining, plantation, railway and manufacturing enterprises in many parts of the world. By the early twentieth century Germany could match Britain as a producer of steel and by 1914 she was not far behind as a producer of coal.

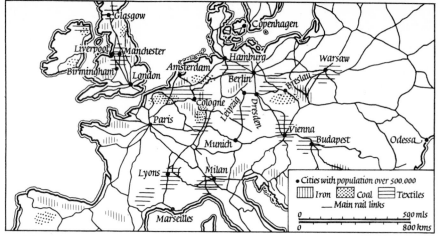

26 Map of central Europe in 1914: coal, iron, textiles and major cities

It was in the period after 1870 that Russia first began to play a significant role in the economic life of Europe. Although possessed of vast resources in raw materials and labour, Russia had been slow to industrialize. The survival of serfdom into the 1860s, a harsh climate, poor roads, few rail links, frozen rivers, a lack of warm-water ports and the remoteness of her coal and iron-ore deposits were all serious handicaps. However, once foreign investment and technical aid had provided some initial momentum, Russia's late start and the unusually active role of the State ensured spectacular progress, but at the same time led to a paradoxical situation. By the early twentieth century Russia could boast a number of large and efficient industrial enterprises quite as advanced as any in Europe, while her great industrial trusts were as large as those of Germany or the United States. Yet side by side with modern collieries, ironworks, engineering plants and textile mills there also existed thousands of small domestic (*kustar*) workshops still persevering with simple tools and hand machines.

Progress in the rest of Europe was rather less rapid than in Britain, Belgium, Germany and Russia. Industrial development in France was steady but unspectacular. The ease with which she paid off her indemnity to Germany after 1871 and the speed with which she recovered from the disastrous effects of the Franco-Prussian War and the Paris Commune showed the

33

underlying strength of her economy. New manufacturing regions were developed under the Third Republic to replace those lost with the German annexation of Alsace-Lorraine. But France's high tariff checked the expansion of her foreign commerce and her shipping and shipbuilding industries. The French electrical and chemical industries could not compete effectively with their German rivals.

Modern industrial centres were developing in Italy north of the Po, in Austria-Hungary in Bohemia and the Vienna district, and in Switzerland, where emphasis was laid on the production of high-quality export goods. But the scale of operations was still comparatively small. Then there were some countries, like Spain, Portugal and Greece in the south and Norway in the north which still had to undergo significant industrial development. Yet it would be fair to say that by 1914 the economy of Europe viewed as a whole had passed through a revolution, for those countries which were not already harvesting the sweet – and bitter – fruits of modern industry were by then irrevocably committed to industrialize as comprehensively and as rapidly as circumstances might allow.

27 Industry in nineteenth-century Sweden: Falun, the country's first industrial town, a copper-mining centre for over six hundred years

28 An epitaph
for the horse

The great era of modern inventions divides into two fairly distinct phases. The first, falling between 1700 and 1850, was dominated by coal, iron and steam, and witnessed the transition from workshop to factory and from individual enterprise to joint-stock company. The second, coinciding with the rise of great firms and trusts from about 1850 onwards, is associated above all with steel, electricity, the internal-combustion engine and the synthesis of new substances, especially in the field of coal-tar derivitives. Both phases demonstrate that, while advances in technology cannot by themselves lead to industrial growth, striking progress can be achieved in a short time if entrepreneurs and skilled artisans have the will and ability to recognize and apply useful new ideas and inventions. During the pioneer phase of British industrialization the chief inventions to capture the imagination of the world were the steam engine, the new textile machines and the new steel-making processes.

THE IRONMASTERS

Early in the eighteenth century the first Abraham Darby of Coalbrookdale discovered how to smelt iron-ore with coke. This was an innovation of great significance, and a timely one, for by 1700 a shortage of timber threatened to bring about a dramatic decline in British pig-iron production. But the discovery was not patented and many years elapsed before it came into general use in British ironworks. Only in the middle of the eighteenth century, when the process was adopted by John Guest at Dowlais and by John Roebuck at Carron, did it become widely known. The slow progress of coke-smelting was perhaps due to the fact that the Darbys were operating a

35

foundry for the production of cast iron and their techniques would therefore not automatically be of interest to ironmasters making bar iron, malleable iron or wrought iron in their forges. The Darby process was improved by John Smeaton, who used cast-iron blowing cylinders to introduce a stronger air current into the blast-furnace in the 1760s, and by J. B. Neilson, who replaced the cold blast with a hot blast in 1828.

The substitution of coal or coke for charcoal in the making of bar iron in the reverberatory furnace appears to have begun in the 1760s on the initiative of the Cranage brothers. In 1783–4 Henry Cort patented the allied puddling and rolling processes. These involved the raking of the molten metal in the reverberatory furnace so that the carbon and other impurities could be separated from the iron, which was then passed through rollers to remove the last of the dross. Peter Onions devised a similar method at about the same time.

The new processes were adopted first in the ironworks of south Wales whence their use spread to other ironworking areas, but they do not seem to have crossed the Channel until after the Napoleonic Wars. Puddling was then introduced into the Seraing ironworks in Belgium, the Hayange ironworks in France, and the Rasselstein and Lendersdorf works in Germany.

A great advance in steel production was made in the 1740s by Benjamin Huntsman of Sheffield, who invented a method of making cast steel by the crucible method. His success lay in making crucibles capable of withstanding great heat and in discovering a suitable flux. Huntsman tried to keep these processes secret, but in 1749 Samuel Walker also produced crucible cast steel. By the late 1780s about twenty Sheffield steel-refiners were making cast steel by the new technique. For some time, however, the process did not spread farther afield. In 1800 David Mushet patented a new method of preparing steel from bar iron by a direct process, and early in the nineteenth century the Swiss metallurgist J. C. Fischer discovered independently how to make crucible cast steel and showed samples at the Berne Industrial Exhibition of 1804. At about the

29 Ironmaster Henry
Cort (1740–1800), in-
ventor of important
iron-refining processes
and 'father' of the
British iron industry

same time Friedrich Krupp of Essen, Poncelet of Liège, and
Andreas Küller of Wald (Solingen) also made cast steel. The
first large plant in France to produce cast steel by the new
process was that established by James Jackson near Saint-Etienne
after the Napoleonic Wars.

THE ARCHITECTS OF THE STEAM AGE

In 1708 a pamphlet entitled *The Compleat Collier* drew attention
to the urgent need to devise more efficient pumps for the
Tyneside coal-mines. A similar problem faced those engaged in
mining tin and copper in Cornwall. A steam pump had already
been patented by Thomas Savery, who had described it in an
earlier pamphlet, *The Miner's Friend* (1702). But the Savery
pump was not powerful enough for the mines, though small
models were used for many years to pump water in private
mansions and pleasure gardens. A few years later Thomas Newcomen invented the more powerful atmospheric engine, and
harnessed it to a pump. The Newcomen steam pump was first
installed on the Wolverhampton-Walsall road in 1712, and from
Staffordshire it spread to other parts of Britain and to the
European mainland. By the 1720s such pumps were operating in

37

Königsberg (in Hungary), Passy (Paris), Londelinsard (near Charleroi), Vienna, Cassel and at the Dannemora mine in Sweden. A Newcomen pump installed at Griff colliery near Coventry is reported to have cost only £150 a year to run, reducing the annual pumping bill by £750.

In the 1760s the Glasgow mechanic James Watt was asked to repair a model of a Newcomen engine. By adding a condenser and a steam pump he turned the atmospheric engine into a genuine steam engine, in which the power was derived from steam and not air pressure. The first Watt engine was used almost exclusively to work pumps. It was more efficient than its predecessor – one model is said to have pumped water three times as quickly as a Newcomen engine – but it was not generally adopted in the coalfields. The Newcomen engine was cheaper to install and its high fuel consumption did not worry the coalowners. The Watt engine was, however, successfully introduced into the Cornish tin-mines.

The ENGINE for Raiſing Water (with a power made) by Fire.

30 The Newcomen atmospheric engine was massive and inefficient, but a boon to eighteenth-century mining. Left, a model built in 1717

31, 32 Plan of the first engine to be powered by steam-pressure and the first to turn a shaft—and its inventor, James Watt (1736–1819)

In 1782 Watt invented a rotary engine, which had a far wider application than his first steam engine, since it could be used to turn a shaft and so drive machinery. While the engine was under patent, the firm of Boulton and Watt built about 200 steam pumps and over 300 rotary engines, and the rapid expansion of the Lancashire industrial district at this time was due, in no small measure, to the application of steam-power to the spinning of cotton. Watt steam engines were also installed in foreign mines – in France at Jary's colliery at Nantes, for example, and in Germany at Hettstett.

When Watt's patent expired in 1800 various new types of steam engine were constructed. Richard Trevithick in England and Oliver Evans in the United States experimented with steam engines which had no condenser and which developed a steam pressure ten times greater than the maximum Watt had considered safe. Other high-pressure engines were built in England by the American engineer Jacob Perkins (1827) and in Germany by Dr Alban (1828), but they were not produced on a commercial scale. Meanwhile, Arthur Woolf of the Hayle foundry improved Trevithick's Cornish engine, which was an efficient pump and popular in the mining districts of south-west England. Woolf's partner, Humphrey Edwards, settled in France and, as manager of the foundry and engineering works established at Chaillot (Paris) by the Perier brothers, built about 200 Woolf compound engines. He also imported Cornish steam pumps for various French mines.

THE SHIP-BUILDERS

Steam-power was applied to transport in the 1780s, when experimental steamships were built in France on the River Saône, in the United States on the Potomac and Delaware, and in Scotland on Loch Dalswinton. After constructing the atmospheric engine for the Dalswinton vessel William Syming-ton was employed by Lord Dundas to build a similar engine for the *Charlotte Dundas*, which sailed on the Forth-Clyde Canal (1801–3). In 1807 Robert Fulton's steamship *Clermont* sailed from New York to Albany on the Hudson; in 1812 Henry Bell inaugurated a daily steamship service on the Clyde; and in 1818 William Denny's *Rob Roy* (fitted with an engine built by David Napier) began a regular service between Glasgow and Belfast. These were wooden paddle-ships. Although John Wilkinson had built an iron barge on the

33 The fate of the *Téméraire* (see ill. 3) heralded a century in advance: design for a steamboat with paddle-wheel, by Jonathan Hull, 1737

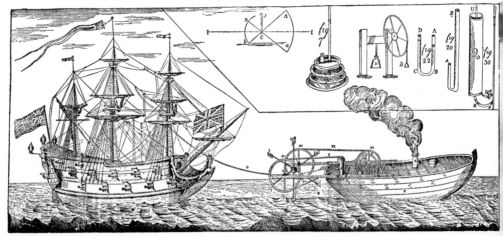

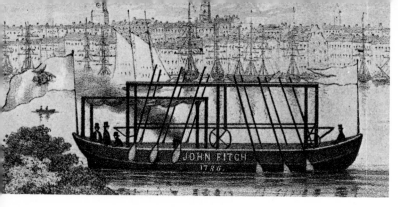

34 John Fitch's experimental steamboat on the Delaware River at Philadelphia, 1786

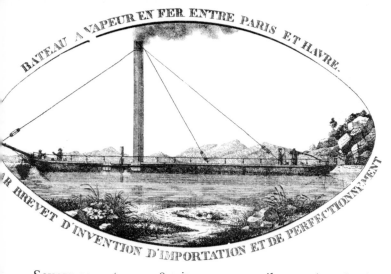

35 London to Paris, 1822. The first iron steamship, *Aaron Manby*

Severn as early as 1787, it was not until 1821 that the first iron steamship, the *Aaron Manby*, appeared. Aaron Manby and his son Charles, having patented a new type of marine engine with oscillating cylinders, built a prefabricated, wrought-iron steamship at Horseley in Staffordshire, assembled it at the Surrey Canal Dock in London and in June 1822 sailed it across the English Channel and up the Seine to Paris. Ten years later, at Birkenhead, John Laird built a second iron steamship for the River Niger trade. In 1836 the first efficient screw-propellers were invented by Sir Francis Pettit-Smith and a Swedish engineer, Captain John Ericsson. But it was not until the 1860s that the superiority of the propeller was clearly established.

41

36, 37 The formidable bow
of the 692-foot *Great Eastern*.
A buoy is being launched
to mark the lie of the trans–
atlantic cable, 1862. Right,
Isambard Kingdom Brunel,
the *Great Eastern*'s co-
designer and promoter,
dwarfed by one of the
vessel's mighty anchor chains

42

In 1858 iron, steam, paddle and screw were wedded in the construction of Isambard Kingdom Brunel's *Great Eastern*, the largest ship of the century. Though performing a useful service by laying transatlantic and other cables it was not a commercial success. Today its hulk can still be seen, aground in the Falkland Islands.

THE RAILWAY PIONEERS

The origin of railways is to be found in colliery tramways. From the sixteenth century onwards, ore had been moved in small hand-carts on parallel planks in the Harz and other mining districts. 'Railways' of this kind appeared in English coal-mines in the seventeenth century. Huntingdon Beaumont laid wooden rails at Wollaton colliery near Nottingham in 1603–4 and at about the same time coal was moved on wooden rails from pits at Broseley to the River Severn. By 1700 many colliery tramways had been laid, the coal normally being transported in wagons hauled by horses.

Between 1768 and 1771 Richard Reynolds of the Coalbrookdale ironworks replaced the wooden rails to Ketley with cast-iron rails having an inner flange. Later rails were made of malleable instead of cast iron and the flange was transferred from the rail to the wheel. Most of the early lines were private railways serving mines, quarries, ironworks, potteries and other industrial establishments. But there were

38 Rails, flanges and positive traction: the pitted iron wheels of Blenkinsop's original locomotive (1812)

43

some public lines such as the Croydon-Wandsworth freight railway and the Swansea-Mumbles passenger railway, both opened in 1804. While railways were quite common in the English mining and industrial districts by the early nineteenth century, few existed elsewhere; and it remained for the French engineer de Gallois-Lachapelle, who visited England after the Napoleonic Wars, to report on the Tyneside colliery railways and strongly recommend the building of such lines in France.

Steam-power was applied to rail transport for the first time in 1804, when a locomotive built by Trevithick ran on an industrial line at Penydarren in south Wales. More successful locomotives were built a few years later for colliery railways by Blenkinsop (1812), Hedley (1813), and George Stephenson (1814). The engines constructed by Stephenson and his son Robert were superior to all others at that time, and the engineering workshops which they set up at Newcastle upon Tyne in 1823 built the locomotives which ran on the first modern railways to be opened in England (1825), Belgium (1835), Germany (1835) and Canada (1836). Within a few years locomotives were also being built in other countries. In France in 1831 a locomotive constructed by Marc Séguin ran on the Saint-Étienne-Lyons line. Two years later Cherepanov and his son built a locomotive to haul wagons in the Nijne-Taguilsh factory in the Urals. In 1839 the *Saxonia*, the first locomotive to be built in Germany, was running on the Dresden-Leipzig line.

44

41 William Hedley's locomotive, *Wylam Dilly*, built in 1813 ▶

◄ 39 An English colliery railway in 1767

40 The great sideshow at Euston Square. Richard Trevithick, inventor of the first steam-powered vehicle to carry a passenger (1801), demonstrates his railway in London, 1809—and profits by its novelty

42 Calico printing, 1835. Roller printing was first successfully applied to textiles in 1735. Previously designs had to be stamped on to the cloth by hand

THE TEXTILE INNOVATORS

The British machines which most impressed contemporaries were those which stimulated the expansion of the cotton industry. In the 1840s a cotton-mill employing 750 workers and using a 100-h.p. steam engine could run 50,000 spindles and produce as much yarn as 200,000 operatives using spinning-wheels; a calico-printing machine operated by one man could print as much cloth in four colours in an hour as 200 men could print by hand. Such machines not only increased output in relation to the number of workers employed, but also enabled substantial reductions in price to be made: cotton yarn cost only 2s 11d per lb in 1832 compared with 38s per lb in 1786. The machines themselves also became cheaper to make; since technical innovations in mines and foundries caused the price of bar iron to fall from £18 per ton in 1750 to between £3 and £4 in 1850. In 1733 John Kay had invented the first important textile device, the fly shuttle, which enabled the hand-loom weaver to double his daily output. He also constructed a machine to make the cards used to disentangle the fibres before spinning. In 1759 one of Kay's sons invented the drop box which enabled a piece of cloth to be woven in three colours nearly as quickly as a length of plain cloth. The acceleration of the weaving process meant that four or five spinners worked to supply a single weaver. So there was every incentive to devise spinning machines to enable a spinner to keep pace with the weaver. In the 1760s James Hargreaves invented the jenny, an improved spinning machine on which a spinner could operate eight spindles instead of one. But the yarn spun by the jenny was suitable only for weft and not for warp, which still had to be spun by the hand wheel. In 1769 Richard Arkwright patented his spinning-frame, which gave the thread a twist by drawing it through rollers. This thread could be used for both weft and warp. Arkwright also devised a method of carding by cylinders.

While the inventions of Kay and Hargreaves were improvements to hand machines, Arkwright's spinning-frame and carding machine were powered first by water and then by steam. Since a single power-unit could drive many machines simultaneously, the adoption of Arkwright's inventions heralded the end of the traditional domestic system of manufacture and the introduction of the factory system.

In 1779 Samuel Crompton invented the mule, which combined the essential features of both jenny and spinning-frame. While this machine greatly increased the output of spinners, weavers continued to use the hand-loom as improved by John Kay and his son. In 1784, however, Edmund Cartwright constructed a power-loom. But, whereas the new spinning machines had been adopted fairly quickly, the transition from hand-loom to power-loom took place slowly. Cartwright's power-loom was a crude and imperfect machine, and numerous improvements had to be made before it could come into general use.

Textile finishing processes were also improved in the last quarter of the eighteenth century. Chlorine-bleaching was introduced by Berthollet, new dyes were discovered, and Thomas Bell invented cylinder printing.

47

The new textile machines were introduced in France and Germany partly by British entrepreneurs and skilled mechanics and partly by local manufacturers. John Kay and his sons lived for many years in France where they made shuttles, card-making machines and other equipment. John Holker, a Jacobite exile who settled in Rouen in 1751, founded a cloth factory at Saint Sever and was appointed Inspector-General of Factories. He introduced the latest cotton machinery and brought over skilled operatives from Lancashire to train French workers in its use. After the Napoleonic Wars English experts, such as Job Dixon and Richard Roberts, helped to bring modern machinery to Alsace, while William Douglas and John Collier introduced new mechanical appliances for the carding, combing and spinning of wool and the shearing of cloth. In Germany three skilled British workers set up a cotton-mill for K. F. Bernhard at Hartau in Saxony in the 1790s, and about twenty years later the younger William Cockerill operated woollen-mills at Guben and Grünberg. Indigenous textile inventions included the Jacquard silk-loom, the Oberkampf-Widmer printing-cylinder, and improved dyeing techniques by Macquer and Berthollet.

THE ENGINEERS

Closely associated with improvements in the production of iron and steel in the eighteenth century were developments in engineering techniques which made possible a great extension of the use of metals. In both civil and mechanical engineering British pioneers led the field. They included the road-builders Metcalf and McAdam and the bridge-builders Telford and Rennie. Then there was George Sorocold, England's leading hydraulic engineer in the early eighteenth century, who built a great waterwheel to drive the silk-mill established by the Lombe brothers at Derby. John Smeaton improved Newcomen's pump, devised a blast-furnace blowing apparatus for the Carron ironworks and built the third Eddystone Lighthouse and the Forth-Clyde Canal. John Wilkinson of

Bersham and Broseley devised a method of boring out cylinders much more accurately than his predecessors, and regularly supplied the firm of Boulton and Watt with steam-engine cylinders. The famous engineering workshops of Boulton and Watt near Birmingham constructed, in addition to steam engines, other machines, such as coin presses. William Murdock, a member of the firm's staff, invented gas lighting.

By the early years of the nineteenth century a new generation of engineers had consolidated Britain's position as world leader in the construction of machines of all kinds. In London, Joseph Bramah invented a wood-planing machine, a hydraulic press, an improved water-closet, a beer-pump, and a new type of lock. Joseph Clement devoted his great talents to the improvement of self-acting tools, particularly the slide-lathe. Henry Maudsley built improved metal lathes fitted with accurate standardized screw-threads and manufactured excellent marine engines. James Nasmyth is remembered for his steam hammer and pile-driver. Marc Isambard Brunel designed over forty steam-driven machines to make wooden pulley blocks for the rigging of naval vessels. He was also responsible for constructing the first tunnel under the Thames, a great feat of civil engineering. John Martineau and his son earned a high reputation for themselves as builders of excellent steam engines, gas generators and pumps.

In Manchester Richard Roberts invented the self-acting mule. Joseph Whitworth constructed precise measuring machines and high-grade machine tools, while his standard screw-thread was adopted all over the world. William Fairbairn was responsible for many improvements in the construction of textile machines and hydraulic machines. He also established a shipbuilding-yard at Millwall (London) for the construction of iron ships, and mechanized the riveting of boiler plates. In Leeds, Matthew Murray introduced important innovations in flax-spinning machinery and invented a heckling machine. He also built the locomotive designed by Blenkinsop, which ran on the Middleton colliery railway.

Peter Fairbairn (William's brother) also improved flax-spinning machinery in Leeds before turning his attention to the armaments industry. In Derby James Fox had a successful career as a constructor of lace-making and planing machines. In Newcastle upon Tyne the Stephensons, father and son, were the leading railway engineers in the country. In Scotland, J. B. Neilson, the manager of the Glasgow gasworks, greatly improved the blast-furnace by inventing the hot blast.

The achievements of British mining engineers led to a sharp rise in the output of the coal, so vital to economic growth during the Industrial Revolution. John Curr of Sheffield increased the efficiency of underground transport by introducing small four-wheeled carts which ran on rails and could be hoisted up the mine-shaft. He laid flanged iron rails, and also invented the flat rope and a method of preventing collisions between carts ascending and descending the shaft. John Buddle of Wallsend introduced the tubbing method of lining shafts with iron castings and modernized mine ventilation and

43 Shop-floor of the Stephenson steam-locomotive factory at Newcastle, 1864. The multi-tubular boiler was patented by Robert Stephenson in 1828

coalworking methods. The rotary engine was adapted to improve pit-head winching efficiency. And the Davy safety lamp reduced the hazards of fire and explosion underground.

A number of British engineers took many of the new inventions and processes across the Channel. Aaron Manby set up engineering workshops at Charenton near Paris and modernized the Le Creusot works. William Jackson at Saint-Etienne and his sons at Assailly also established modern engineering works in France. William Cockerill set up a plant for the construction of textile machines at Verviers in Belgium, while his son John founded the famous engineering establishment at Seraing near Liège. British engineers and contractors also assisted in the construction of railways, such as the line from Paris to Rouen.

However, the careers of men like Héron de Villefosse, A. H. de Bonnard, L. A. Beaunier, Louis de Gallois-Lachapelle and Marc Séguin show that France possessed her own very talented engineers in the early nineteenth century. Séguin was the first French engineer to build a railway, a locomotive and a suspension bridge; and high standards of workmanship were attained in the ironworks and engineering plants of the Perier brothers at Chaillot, the de Wendels at Hayange, Dufaud at Fourchambault, the Schneider brothers at Le Creusot, Dietrich at Niederbronn and Thierry-Mieg at Mulhouse. In Switzerland Hans Caspar Escher and his son operated a plant at Zürich for the construction of textile machinery which was one of the most efficient in Europe. In Germany in the early nineteenth century Franz Dinnendahl and Fritz Harkort were among the earliest machine-builders in the Ruhr; F. A. J. Egells established a modern iron-foundry and engineering works in Berlin; Ferdinand Schichau constructed machinery and, later, steamships, at Elbing; while Georg von Reichenbach made his reputation as an accurate constructor of scientific instruments. The coming of railways led to the establishment of a number of locomotive-works in Germany, the most important being those of Borsig in Berlin, Klett in Nuremberg, Egestorff in Hanover, Henschel in Cassel, and Hartmann in Chemnitz.

New advances in technology were made in the second half of the nineteenth century. The age of steel was heralded by the Bessemer and Siemens–Martin process, the age of electricity by Werner Siemen's dynamo and electric tram, the age of the motor car by Otto's gas engine, and the age of modern chemistry by Perkin's first aniline dye and Solvay's ammonia process for making soda. Britain, which had dominated the earlier period of inventions, still made important contributions, such as the Bessemer steel converter, the Gilchrist-Thomas basic steel process, and the Parsons steam turbine; but a great many technical advances were now originating in other European countries.

THE INDUSTRIAL CHEMISTS

With the appearance of the scientific research team working in an expensive laboratory, the days of the inventor in his private workshop were numbered. The case of Friedrich Bayer & Co. of Elberfeld, a German firm founded in the early 1860s by Bayer and Weskutt to manufacture the recently discovered aniline dyes, illustrates this development. Between 1864 and 1874 four foremen, trained at the Krefeld Textile Trade School, shared responsibility for both research and production. But as dyeing processes became more sophisticated the firm began to appreciate the need to employ talented chemistry graduates to carry out research projects. The most outstanding chemist to be appointed was Carl Duisberg, who discovered three new dyes in 1884–6. He was able to devote all his time to research, and soon had a dozen assistants working under him. In 1890 the firm decided to invest £750,000 in a new laboratory and library for Duisberg and his colleagues. Duisberg now divided his time between the organization of research teams, which were expected to discover new dyes and processes, and the vocational training of all chemists joining the firm. As F. Bayer & Co. extended its interests to include the manufacture of new chemical products, such as heavy chemicals, medicines, ointments and photographic accessories, so the work of Duisberg's laboratories expanded. It was common for German chemical firms to maintain contact with the chemistry departments of particular universities, and Duisberg cemented close links between his research workers and the chemistry departments of Berlin and Würzburg Universities.

Progress in the manufacture of chemicals was stimulated by the growth of the textile, soap and glass industries and by the expansion of agriculture, which brought with it an ever increasing demand for dyestuffs, alkalis and fertilizers. New substances were synthesized, new manufacturing methods devised and old methods improved. Soda, formerly made from the ashes of barilla or kelp, was later produced by Leblanc, who heated sodium sulphate, limestone and charcoal together, and by Solvay, who passed carbonic acid through a solution of salt saturated with ammonia. Dyes, formerly made from natural substances, came to be manufactured from coal-tar derivatives. In 1856 W. H. Perkin produced a synthetic mauve dye – the first of the aniline dyes – and Notanson produced magenta. Cloths impregnated with brilliantly coloured aniline

44, 45 Sir Henry Bessemer (1813–98), who made steel by passing a blast of air through molten cast-iron. Right, a Bessemer converter in Germany, 1865

dyes were much admired at the industrial exhibitions held in London in 1862 and in Paris in 1867. Later German chemists produced a number of other new coal-tar dyes. For example, in 1869 Graebe and Liebermann prepared alizarin, the colouring matter of the madder root, from anthracene.

Progress in other branches of the chemical industry was equally spectacular. In the 1860s the Swedish inventor Alfred Nobel discovered the explosive qualities of nitro-glycerine and the principle of sympathetic detonation; he became a manufacturer of dynamite and blasting gelatine. In the field of 'fine' chemicals – drugs and cosmetics, for example – important basic research had been carried out in England and France in the late eighteenth and early nineteenth centuries, but after 1870 German chemists greatly extended the range of practical

46, 47 Left, Liebig's laboratory at Giessen, 1842. One product of nineteenth-century chemistry was the photograph. Above, self-portrait of pioneer photographer and aeronaut Nadar, 1856

applications to which these discoveries could be put. The development of plastics was a major advance. The first modern thermoplastics (seals, gramophone records, beer-stoppers) were made from materials such as natural resins and waxes, but in 1865 Alexander Parkes of Birmingham produced the first synthetic thermoplastic, from celluloid. In 1872 the first coal-tar – or thermosetting – plastic was discovered by Bayer, and shortly after the turn of the century the Belgian chemist L. H. Baekeland succeeded in synthesizing the bakelite resins, an important new group of coal-tar plastics. The specific study of the application of chemistry to agriculture was initiated by Justus Liebig at Giessen, and large deposits of potassium salts found at Stassfurt-Leopoldshall were shown by Rudolf Frank's researches to be valuable fertilizers.

48 Marconi with his apparatus for 'telegraphy without wires', 1896

THE ELECTRICAL TECHNOLOGISTS

Electrical and magnetic phenomena had been closely studied in the eighteenth century. In 1797 the Italian physicist Volta proved the existence of current – as distinct from static – electricity and a little later showed that electricity could be generated by a chemical reaction in a battery. Russian scientists experimented with batteries in attempting to produce electric light and traction. Petrov's battery – an 'enormous pile comprising 4,200 copper and zinc washers' – was described in a book published in St Petersburg in 1803. In 1834 B. S. Jacobi used batteries to drive an electric 'engine' installed in a boat. In 1820 Oersted found that an electric current produces a magnetic field, and in 1832 Faraday discovered the principle of the dynamo, which enabled him to convert mechanical energy into electrical power.

Electricity was first put to practical use when telegraphs were constructed in the 1830s in Germany by Gauss and Weber, in America by Morse, and in England by Wheatstone and Cooke. It was not until the 1860s, when efficient dynamos were built by Antonio Pacinotti and Werner Siemens and harnessed to steam engines, waterwheels and turbines, that it became possible to use electricity for lighting, transport and industrial power. Electric lighting developed when the filament lamp was invented by Swan in England and Edison in America (1878–9). Effective electric traction was achieved in the 1880s when Werner Siemens built an electric tram to run in the streets of a Berlin suburb, while his brother, William, constructed an electric railway at Portrush. Underground electric railways were opened in London, Budapest and Boston in the 1890s.

The earliest large electric generating stations were those built by Edison in New York and by Ferranti in London. The first electric cable to transmit power over a long distance was opened between Lauffen on the River Neckar and Frankfurt am Main in 1891. The great advantage of the electric generator over the steam engine could now be clearly demonstrated. While the energy derived from a steam engine had to be used on the spot, the power produced by an electric generator could be used many miles away.

Meanwhile experiments in England by Wheatstone and in Germany by Reis paved the way for the development of the telephone by Bell and Edison in the United States. A spectacular advance in communications technology came at the end of the nineteenth century when the Italian engineer Marconi devised an apparatus by which electromagnetic waves, discovered earlier by Maxwell and Hertz, could be used to transmit messages. The British Post Office provided facilities for the development of this invention to the point at which it could be used effectively, while similar experiments in wireless telegraphy were conducted by A. S. Popov in St Petersburg.

THE MOTOR-CAR DESIGNERS

The invention of the internal-combustion engine – like the invention of the electric generator – provided the industrial societies of Europe and the United States with a valuable new source of power. The first gas engines were built in the 1860s in Germany and France by Lenoir, Beau de Rochas, Hugon and N. A. Otto, and the first engineering plant to make small petrol motors was established at Deutz (near Cologne) by

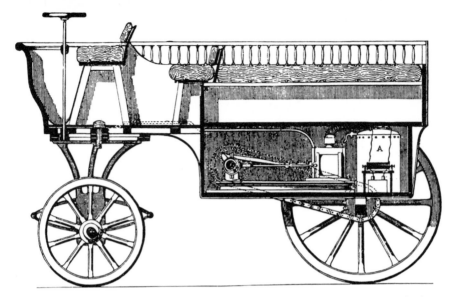

49 Above, Lenoir's car (1860). Its engine, powered by the combustion of a low-pressure mixture of inflammable gas and air, was slow-acting and inefficient

Otto and Langen. In 1872 the latter were joined by Gottlieb Daimler and Wilhelm Maybach, and before long the firm was turning out a four-stroke engine. As early as 1875 Franz Reuleaux declared that the little gas engine would become 'the real power-machine of the masses'.

The new engine was applied to transport by Daimler and Maybach (who established a firm of their own at Cannstatt in 1882) and by Karl Benz (who built an independent petrol engine of his own at Mannheim). In 1885 both firms built motor cars which were demonstrated to the public. Daimler also fitted his engine to a boat which sailed on the Seine during the Paris Exhibition of 1887. In 1894 Karl Benz produced a cheap popular car. Called a 'Velo', it cost £100, and could travel at twelve miles per hour. The engineering firm of Panhard and Levassor secured Daimler's French patent rights and began to build their own vehicles with such vigour that by 1900 France was the leading manufacturer of motor cars in Europe.

50, 51, 52 The invention of the high-speed internal-combustion engine gave birth to the modern motor industry. Far left, Karl Benz at the wheel of his motor car of 1887. Left, Wilhelm Maybach steering the first Daimler four-wheeler. Below, the first motorcycle, built by Daimler in 1885

53, 54 Rudolph Diesel (1858–1913) and advertisement, 1897. Instead of a spark, Diesel's engine used the heat generated by compressed air to ignite the fuel mixture

In the 1890s the German manager of an ice factory in Paris, Rudolph Diesel, invented the Diesel engine.

AMERICAN INVENTORS

Inventions in the United States also played a part in the industrial development of Europe. Shortage of skilled workers in New England and other manufacturing districts encouraged the invention of labour-saving devices and the development of innovations which had been neglected in Europe. As early as the middle of the nineteenth century two English official visitors to an industrial exhibition in New York reported that they had seen a 'machine for the manufacture of seamless grain-bags, the loom for which is described as a perfect self-actor or automaton, commencing the bag, and continuing the process until the work is turned out complete'. In the cotton industry the Brooks-Doxey ringframe and the Northrop automatic loom were among the most important inventions since those of Arkwright and Roberts. The clothing and foot-wear industries were revolutionized by the sewing machine, which was invented by Elias Howe in 1846 and improved by Singer in 1852. Edison, the greatest American inventor, was remarkably prolific in electrical and chemical innovations. The typewriter was an American invention. And many of the most significant improvements in agricultural machinery in the nineteenth century, such as the McCormick reaper, the Marsh harvester and the twine-binder, were American in origin.

Why the eighteenth century should have given birth to a sudden spark of important inventions, has been the subject of much conjecture and debate. It has been argued that inventions generally appear in response to a need for a new or improved technique. For example, the discovery that charcoal could be replaced by coal or coke as a smelting agent was undoubtedly hastened by a timber shortage in Britain. Similarly, an acute shortage of Huntsman crucible cast steel in Napoleonic Europe, and the incentive of a prize offered in France, would have been powerful inducements to Poncelet of Liège and Fischer of Schaffhausen to rediscover the method of making such steel. And when, a little later, Napoleon offered a substantial reward for the invention of an improved flax-spinning machine, such a machine was shortly afterwards constructed by Philippe de Girard.

Events in Lancashire in 1824 showed how a new machine could be invented to meet a crisis. A strike of cotton operatives appeared to endanger the future of Britain's major export industry, and, according to Andrew Ure, three leading mill-owners approached Richard Roberts and asked him if he could construct a machine to make the spinning mules run out and in at the proper speed by means of self-acting machinery, and thus render them in some measure independent of the more refractory of their workmen. Roberts thereupon invented the self-acting mule, which eventually met the requirements of the millowners. Samuel Smiles observes that several other important inventions were prompted by labour disputes which led manufacturers to seek machines to replace strikers.

It has also been pointed out that inventions in one industry may stimulate inventions in another. T. S. Ashton observes that 'the principles of alternating material by passing it through

55 A jaundiced view of the inventor, and a prophetic essay on the ambivalence of techno-logical progress. Daumier's cartoon, *The Dream of the Inventor of the Needle Gun* (1866)

rollers was transferred from the iron to the textile industry' and that 'Wilkinson's method of boring cannon was turned to the making of steam-engine cylinders.'

Certain innovations were the culmination of the efforts of successive inventors attempting to solve the same problem: Arkwright's water-frame of 1769 had been anticipated some thirty years before by Lewis Paul and John Wyatt, who had constructed a roller-spinning machine; Watt's steam engine had been preceded by the atmospheric engine of Newcomen; while Otto's gas engines had been preceded by that of Lenoir. Moreover, as Samuel Smiles points out, 'many inventions appear to be coincident. . . . A number of minds are working at the same time in the same track, with the object of supplying some want generally felt; and, guided by the same experi-ence, they not infrequently arrive at like results. It has some-times happened that the inventors have been separated by great distances, so that piracy on the part of either was impos-sible.' The puddling process in the iron industry, as we have seen, was invented almost simultaneously by Cort and Onions; and in the 1780s the first steamships sailed in Britain and in America within a few years of each other. In the early days of the locomotive George Stephenson's *Blücher* was not the only engine in daily use on colliery lines. Hedley's *Puffing Billy* and *Wylam Dilly* and Blenkinsop's locomotive were in operation at the same time. In 1828 a multi-tubular locomotive boiler was patented by Robert Stephenson and Henry Booth in England and by Marc Séguin in France. In 1836 marine propellers were patented by Ericsson and Pettit-Smith. In the 1830s the electric telegraph appeared simultaneously in England, Germany and the United States. Wool-combing machines were invented by Heilmann in France in 1845 and by Donisthorpe, Lister and Holden in England shortly afterwards. In the 1840s Mayer in Germany, Fischer in Switzerland and Anusov in Russia all discovered how to make steel castings. In 1878 the electric thread-filament was invented simultaneously in England and the United States. In 1885 the first motor cars were built at Canstatt by Daimler and Maybach and at Mannheim by Benz. And in 1895 the earliest moving pictures were shown by the Lumière brothers in Paris and by the Schadanowsky brothers in Berlin.

A striking feature of the Industrial Revolution in the eighteenth century, particularly in Britain, was the number of inventions and innovations that were made by ingenious craftsmen who constructed new machines or discovered new processes, not by the application of scientific principles but by the method of trial and error. Newcomen was a blacksmith and ironmonger, Crompton a spinner, Brindley a wheelwright, Neilson and Rennie millwrights, Clement a slater, Telford a stone-mason, Metcalf a horse-dealer, and Hargreaves a weaver. Although Watt's initial experiments were made in association with Professor Black of Glasgow University, the steam engine was a rule-of-thumb development, and when Carnot put forward the first theory of the heat engine in 1824 it was ignored by the engineers of his day.

But side by side with the artisan-inventors there were better-educated innovators who were aware of advances in technical knowledge and were in close touch with scientists. Roebuck, for example, studied at Leyden University, while Davy and Faraday were scientific research workers as well as practical inventors. Later, in the great age of German technical advance, the inventors who contributed so much to the development of the motor car and the new electrical and chemical industries were generally men who had been trained at universities or technical colleges. These inventors were aware of the links between advances in science and progress in technology. In England the Royal Society (1660), the Royal Society of Arts (1754) and the Royal Institution (1800) promoted both scientific and technical researches while the mechanics institutes provided a general education in practical subjects. In France the College of Highways and Bridges (1747), the College of Mines (1793) and the Polytechnic (1794) gave a sound training for engineers. In Germany mining academies had been established at Freiberg and Clausthal in 1765. Early in the nineteenth century the Prussian government established a Technical Commission and a Technical Institute in Berlin, while royal patronage was extended to the Association for the Promotion of Technical Knowledge. Institutions of this kind either provided facilities for technical training or fostered collaboration between scientists, technologists and laymen.

The activities of such bodies in many European countries indicate the presence of an intellectual and social climate favourable to scientific and technical progress. Where there was a less favourable environment inventors made relatively little progress. In Russia, for example, Glinkov's flax-spinning machine, Polzunov's atmospheric engine, Anusov's cast-steel process, Cherepanov's locomotive, Jacobi's electromagnetic telegraph, Kouzminsky's turbine and Zvorykin's remarkable discoveries concerning the mechanics of cutting metals did not gain the recognition they would have earned in a more advanced manufacturing country.

III THE ENTREPRENEURS

56 Absorbed in his enterprise, *The Railway King*; a Victorian caricature

PUBLIC ENTERPRISE

The governments of European countries employed various expedients to initiate and hasten the progress of industrialization. On the one hand they sought to provide an environment as favourable as possible to the expansion of manufacturing enterprise. This policy of indirect encouragement to industry generally entailed the freeing of serfs; the abolition of the medieval privileges of guilds and municipalities; the removal or reduction of tolls on rivers and roads; the provision of a sound currency based upon silver or gold; the maintenance of a national central bank; the construction of public works (roads, canals, railways) and public utilities (harbours, waterworks, gasworks); the application of protective tariffs and colonial preferences, and the enforcement of a navigation code to safeguard shipping and shipbuilding interests. It also involved the recruiting of skilled craftsmen from abroad, the prohibition of both the emigration of skilled artisans and the export of machinery and blueprints, the protection of inventions by a patent law, the payment of subsidies to encourage industrial output and promote exports, the regulation of freight charges on railways and canals, the founding of technical colleges, and the holding of industrial exhibitions.

65

57 The Crystal Palace, originally built in Hyde Park to house Prince Albert's successful Great Exhibition of 1851, re-erected at Sydenham, 1854

It was not always possible for governments to provide the favourable conditions they desired. During the French Revolution the depreciation of the currency by issuing *assignats* was one of the factors which retarded industrial growth at that time. And for much of the nineteenth century the Russian rouble was a notoriously unstable currency. After the Napoleonic Wars the Royal Bank of Berlin was so heavily in debt that it could not fulfil the normal functions of a central bank, and at the same time the disorganized condition of both national and local finances in nearly all the German States prevented them from carrying out urgently needed programmes of public works. In France in 1818 a report by the eminent engineer Louis de Gallois-Lachapelle complained of the lack of colliery railways while six years later F. L. Becquey, Director-General of the Department of Highways and Bridges, stated that the

58 The 'Palace of Electricity', a fantastic pavilion at the Paris Exhibition of 1900—an exhibition which attracted some thirty-nine million visitors

French roads were in a deplorable condition, and that industrialized regions such as the district around Lyons and Saint-Etienne had the worst roads of all. Moreover the effectiveness of government encouragement depended upon the quality of the civil service and in many countries this left something to be desired.

It may be argued that some governments, despite their good intentions hindered rather than promoted industrial growth by the very thoroughness of their attempts to regulate manufactures. There can be little doubt that in the first half of the nineteenth century the Prussian mining code, which gave government inspectors extensive powers to regulate the day-to-day working of collieries and other mines, checked the flow of capital into the industry and so retarded its development. Similarly, the centralized French system of bureaucratic

67

59 'You've never had it so good.' Bureaucrat, and Bourbon reactionary at heart, Louis-Philippe (1773–1850) courted popular favour with empty gestures. In practice, he opposed social reforms essential to France's industrial progress

control over industry and public building during the Restoration and the reign of Louis-Philippe may well have been one of the factors which slowed down industrial growth.

Governments also intervened directly, by creating a public sector of the economy. In Britain this was done to a very limited extent only, but elsewhere either the State itself, public corporations, or local authorities owned or controlled mines, railways and manufacturing enterprises. Government interests included collieries, ironworks, saltworks, arsenals, dockyards, textile mills, flour-mills, porcelain-works, tapestry-works, and many others. Some of these had been founded in the seventeenth and eighteenth centuries, long before the age of modern manufactures, and grew from workshops in which simple appliances were used into factories with steam-driven machinery. Others, like the nationalized coal-mines and railways of the nineteenth century, were established to meet the needs of the new industrial era.

Motives for establishing State enterprises were varied. The maintenance of arsenals and naval dockyards was necessary in the interests of national defence. Certain factories, like some State farms, were model establishments, intended to give a lead to private enterprise by installing the most up-to-date machinery and production techniques. Some nationalized factories were set up in regions where old-established industries were declining in order to provide work for the unemployed. The establishment of State mines, factories and railways in the nineteenth century was carried out by governments holding very different political opinions, but rarely influenced by socialist doctrines. The work of Motz, Beuth and Rother in Prussia, of Napoleon III in France and of Count Witte in Russia will serve to illustrate the role of government in greater detail.

PRUSSIA: FRIEDRICH VON MOTZ

In 1815 few observers could have foreseen that by 1900 Germany would have become the leading industrial country on the European mainland: economic progress was hampered by adverse geographical and political conditions; the main coalfields lay on the periphery of the country and could not be adequately exploited until railways were built; before the age of steam, Hamburg and Bremen could not compete successfully with Liverpool or Le Havre on the Atlantic trade routes; lack of capital and poor transport facilities checked economic growth; and the division of the country into many independent States, each in complete control of its own economic policy, hampered the development of internal commerce. Prussia, the largest of the north German States, had made substantial territorial gains in 1815, but it was not easy to mould her eastern and western provinces into an economic unit, since they were separated by the lands of other German States. The Napoleonic Wars had left a legacy of heavy debts which prevented the government from pursuing as active an economic policy as it would have wished. But after her defeat at Jena, Prussia, under the guidance of Stein and Hardenberg, had embarked upon a great programme of reforms to modernize

69

the country's institutions, and established an economic tradition that was continued by various Prussian officials after 1815.

When Friedrich von Motz became Minister of Finance in 1825 he realized that if Prussia were to develop her industries it would be necessary for the country to become a free-trade area. In addition the Prussian customs area would have to include various enclaves from which foreign goods were being smuggled into the country, as well as sufficient territories from other German States to provide a link between the country's eastern and western provinces. By 1825 several enclaves had already agreed to enter the new tariff area, but the Duke of Anhalt-Köthen, ruler of a miniature State on the River Elbe, refused to do so until 1828 when, under threat of blockade, he submitted. By 1830 the problem of the enclaves had been solved.

It proved much more difficult to establish a link between Prussia's two separate groups of provinces so that trade could move freely throughout the kingdom. At first Motz's efforts to form a north German customs union failed. Hanover and the other States which he approached feared that any form of economic union with Prussia would eventually bring them under the political domination of their powerful neighbour. All that Motz had achieved by 1828 was the formation of a customs union with Hesse-Darmstadt. Although this made a useful link between the Rhineland province and Bavaria it still provided no contact between the eastern and western parts of Prussia. Moreover, this union so alarmed the central and northern States of Germany that they established the Middle German Commercial Union, under the leadership of Hanover and Saxony, and pledged themselves to refrain from joining any other union before 1835.

Motz did not allow this setback to deter him, however, for he realized that, owing to the mutual jealousies of the smaller German States, the bark of the Middle German Commercial Union was worse than its bite. The Union planned to link Hamburg and Bremen with Leipzig and Frankfurt am Main

60 Friedrich von Motz (1775–1830),
architect of the Zollverein

by roads which would avoid Prussian territory and obviate
the need to pay Prussian transit dues. But the scheme was not
carried out because the States concerned could not agree
among themselves on the precise routes to be followed. Motz
then successfully adopted the very method that the Middle
German Commercial Union had hoped to use against Prussia.
The Prussian government began to build new roads linking
the territories of the Prussia-Hesse-Darmstadt customs union
with those of the recently formed Bavaria-Württemberg
customs union – roads that passed through the territories of
various small Thuringian States which were members of the
Middle German Commercial Union. If these States had whole-
heartedly supported the policy of the Union they would have
refused Prussia access. In 1829 Meiningen and Coburg agreed,
in return for subsidies and loans, that Prussia might build roads
through their territories, and five months later the Reuss
Principalities followed suit. In the same year Motz successfully completed negotiations with the Dutch government to
facilitate navigation on the Rhine; Holland ceased to levy
the transit dues formerly charged at the mouths of the Rhine,
Leck and Waal, and also gave up the monopoly enjoyed by
Dutch shipping guilds, while the German river-ports of
Cologne, Mainz and Mannheim gave up their staple rights.
By securing these concessions Prussia demonstrated her capacity
and willingness to act as spokesman for the whole of Germany
in important commercial negotiations.

71

61, 62 Peter Beuth (1781–1853), Prussian civil servant, and a locomotive named in his honour, built by Borsig of Berlin in 1844

PRUSSIA: PETER BEUTH

While Motz, who died suddenly in 1830, was laying the foundations of the Zollverein, another Prussian, Peter Beuth, was devoting his energies to the modernization of his country's industries. Between 1818 and 1845 Beuth was in charge of the Department of Industry and Trade in the Ministry of Finance. He saw that Prussia was on the threshold of the machine age and was determined to do all in his power to hasten the transition. He had little sympathy with those who opposed rapid technical advance for fear of unemployment among domestic craftsmen. He admired men like the silk-manufacturer Georg Gabain who built up a large industrial enterprise in Berlin on his own initiative, but he realized that in Prussia many entrepreneurs required some encouragement and assistance from the State. Appreciating the fact that Prussia had much to learn from more advanced industrial regions, Beuth twice crossed the Channel in the 1820s to see for himself what technical progress had already been achieved in Britain. He also travelled to Belgium and France to inspect the engineering works of John Cockerill and Aaron Manby. He visited the

72

63 Indulging the iron horse: a typical scene at August Borsig's foundry and engineering works, Berlin, 1850 ▶

industrial regions of Prussia to inspect factories and workshops and to urge their owners to use the most advanced methods and machinery available, and he encouraged promising young men, such as the locksmith F. A. J. Egells, to seek further knowledge and experience abroad.

Beuth tried to improve the efficiency of Prussia's industries not only through the government department for which he was responsible but also through other organizations – the Technical Commission, the Technical Institute, and the Association for the Promotion of Technical Knowledge in Prussia. The Technical Commission, founded in 1810 and reorganized in 1819, when Beuth became its director, was an official body which administered the patent law and promoted the writing of textbooks on scientific and technical subjects. Beuth was also Director of the Berlin Technical Institute, established in 1821 to provide a two-year training course for boys over the age of twelve. The number of scholars rose from 13 in 1821 to 101 in 1845 and eventually the Institute developed into the Charlottenberg Technical College. Borsig, the builder of some of Germany's earliest locomotives, and Schichau, who constructed Germany's first steam-dredger and first iron screw-propelled steamship, were former students of the Technical Institute.

64 Bucolic view of the port of Hamburg from across the Elbe, 1830

The Association for the Promotion of Technical Knowledge in Prussia was founded in 1820. It was a private organization but its statutes received the approval of the government. It grew out of informal gatherings of men from many different walks of life – civil servants, army officers, manufacturers, scientists and artists – who met on Sunday afternoons in Beuth's house. Beuth was elected chairman of the Association, which held regular meetings to discuss problems of improving industrial efficiency, and published transactions concerning advances in technology at home and abroad. The three organizations founded by Beuth were all accommodated in the House of Industry in the Klosterstrasse in Berlin. There Beuth had his official residence and there he established a library and an important collection of machines and models.

PRUSSIA: CHRISTIAN VON ROTHER

A third public servant who played an important part in promoting industrial expansion in Prussia after the Napoleonic Wars was Christian von Rother. For many years he was head of the Overseas Trading Corporation (Seehandlung) and the National Debt Redemption Office; in 1837 he was

74

65 Hamburg from the same vantage point, 1910 ▶

also placed in charge of the Royal Bank of Berlin. The See-handlung was a public corporation which had been founded by Frederick the Great in 1772 to stimulate trade in the valley of the Vistula, after West Prussia had been annexed by Prussia. It acquired an additional function as a financial institution to raise government loans. Both of these functions were retained by the Seehandlung after its reorganization by Rother in the 1820s. Rother had already established his reputation as a financier by negotiating a £5 million loan for the Prussian government with Nathan Rothschild in London, and in 1822 he raised a second loan of £3 million from the same source. Some of this money was used to finance industrial projects and to build roads. Rother's prudent administration of the national debt enabled him to reduce it by 68 million thalers between 1820 and 1843. As soon as the immediate financial needs of the government had been met by the London loans, Rother endeavoured to find new markets for Prussian manufactured goods. He was particularly anxious to revive the linen exports of his native province of Silesia where many hand-loom weavers were finding it difficult to make a living. In 1822 a Seehandlung vessel which he had sent to Rio de Janeiro laden with linen cloth returned with a consignment of coffee, sugar

and cotton. Next he sent William O'Swald on two voyages round the world to sell Prussian linens. Eventually a regular service of Seehandlung ships was established between Hamburg and the West Indies, South America, India and China. The Corporation also traded heavily in wool, flour and alum.

The Seehandlung fostered internal communications by building 600 miles of highways, by maintaining river steamship services in the province of Brandenburg, and by purchasing shares in the Berlin-Anhalt Railway Company, and in an engineering plant which was established at Dirschau in preparation for the construction of the Berlin-Königsberg Railway. Factories owned or managed by the Seehandlung included a woollen-spinning mill at Breslau, a power-loom weaving shed at Wüste Giersdorf, four flax-spinning mills in Silesia, and a cotton factory near Glatz. The corporation operated zinc-rolling mills at Ohlau, an iron-foundry at Burgthal and engineering works in Berlin and Breslau, a chemical factory at Oranienburg, paper-mills in Berlin and Hohenofen, and an important group of factories at Bromberg. Since most of these factories lay east of the River Elbe and were situated in remote country districts, they provided new employment for rural workers formerly engaged in declining crafts.

Rother was also responsible for an important reform of the Prussian banking system. In the 1840s Prussian manufacturers, especially those in the Rhineland and Westphalia, were pressing the government to establish a central bank, permit the founding of joint-stock credit banks, and expand the note issue. Rother had been placed in charge of the affairs of the Royal Bank of Berlin and succeeded in reorganizing it completely. It became the Bank of Prussia with a capital of 11 million thalers, of which 10 million were subscribed by private shareholders. But the influence of the shareholders on the management of the bank was strictly limited and real power lay in the hands of a committee appointed by the King. The new bank issued notes to the value of 21 million thalers, one-third of which had to be covered by bullion.

66 Napoleon III (1808–73), who saw in the industrial reconstruction of France the key to national prosperity and a way of safeguarding his own personal power. He believed that a policy of vigorous state action was necessary to ensure rapid industrial growth

In France the economic policy of Louis Napoleon showed how a dynamic ruler could stimulate private entrepreneurs to greater exertions than before. The reorganization of the railway system, the rebuilding of central Paris, the construction of public works in provincial cities, the building of new harbours, the government loan to manufacturers, the encouragement of new credit banks of industry and agriculture, the radical reform of the tariff initiated by the Cobden-Chevalier Treaty, and the holding of two important international exhibitions in Paris all helped to promote the growth of French industry during his reign. The Emperor was served by able administrators such as Eugène Rouher, G. E. Haussmann, P. J. Bairoch and Franqueville. His letter to his Minister Fould, issued at the time of the signing of the treaty of commerce with Britain, strongly suggests that he was following out a policy of carefully co-ordinated economic measures.

Between the end of the Napoleonic Wars and the fall of the Second Republic the industrial development of France proceeded at a much slower pace than that of Britain or Belgium. Few French manufacturing centres expanded as rapidly as Birmingham, Manchester, Leeds or Liège. There was little

77

evidence of growth in the output of coal, pig iron or textiles, in the construction of railways, or in the volume of foreign and colonial trade. France's resources of coal did not match those of England or Germany. She did have large iron-ore deposits in Lorraine but they were not adequately exploited until the province was annexed by Germany in 1871, and the discovery of the Gilchrist-Thomas process enabled steel to be made from the phosphoric *minette* ore of the region. It was rare for coal and iron to be found close together in France.

The growth of some of France's major ports, such as Marseilles and Bordeaux, was retarded by lack of adequate industrial hinterlands. Losses of territory in Canada and India in the eighteenth century had curtailed opportunities for colonial trade, while the severance of France's commercial contacts with the eastern Mediterranean during the Napoleonic Wars adversely affected the fortunes of Marseilles. France's outstanding industrial achievements were in luxury trades – the production of artistic high-quality products such as silks, cambrics, carpets, glassware and porcelain – and not in mass-produced goods for which England was famous. The French luxury industries catered for wealthy customers, and manufactures of this type proved to be particularly susceptible to unpredictable changes in fashion and to the fluctuations of the trade cycle.

Napoleon III realized the importance of communications in promoting industrial growth and was determined to provide France with an efficient railway system. A law passed in Louis-Philippe's reign had laid down the routes of future trunk-lines and had provided that railways should be constructed by private enterprise in association with the State. The government defrayed the cost of the 'infrastructure' – the land, the roadbed, cuttings, bridges, tunnels – while the companies were responsible for laying and maintaining track, constructing stations, and providing locomotives, wagons, coaches and signals. The State sometimes gave additional help to railway companies by purchasing shares or granting loans. In 1848 the capital sum spent on the railways amounted to 955 million francs of which 331 million had been contributed by the State. Since the government had a substantial financial stake in the railways, it was anxious that the system should quickly be completed and start paying its way.

Under the Second Empire the State granted ninety-nine-year concessions to railway companies, and guaranteed the interest on many of their shares. Above all it encouraged – sometimes compelled – railway companies to amalgamate so that one major line would serve each geographical region in the country. In the five years after 1852 some 15,000 kilometres of track had been laid and the number of companies reduced to six: the Northern Railway linked Paris with the industries of Lille, the collieries of Valenciennes, and the trade of the Channel ports; the Paris-Orleans-Bordeaux line served the Loire Valley; the P. L. M. (Paris-Lyon-Mediterranée) Railway served the Valley of the Rhône; the Eastern Railway (Paris-Strasbourg-Basel) linked the capital with the province of Alsace; the Western Railway ran from Paris to Rouen, Le Havre and Cherbourg; and the Midi Railway served the hinterland of Bordeaux.

The amalgamations had hardly been completed when the great commercial crisis of 1857 made it extremely difficult for railway companies to raise public money for new lines which they were under an obligation to construct. The government therefore negotiated new agreements with the six companies and, under the Railway Law of 1859, guaranteed investors interest on the new lines. To assist those in difficulties it taxed the more profitable lines and in this way many railway shares became virtually as safe as government bonds. By 1870 nearly 18,000 kilometres of track had been laid, not only providing France with an efficient transport system, but also giving direct employment to railway personnel and the many hundreds of workers engaged by the contractors, and indirect employment to workers in ironworks, sawmills, brickworks and many other industrial establishments.

69 Demolition of part of the Latin Quarter in the course of the reconstruction of Paris. Although alive to the economic advantages of broad boulevards, Napoleon was also motivated by the thought that, in the event of civil disorder, they would be much harder to barricade than narrow streets ▶

67 Baron Georges Haussmann (1809–91), Prefect of the Seine Department, charged by Napoleon III in 1853 with the beautification of the capital

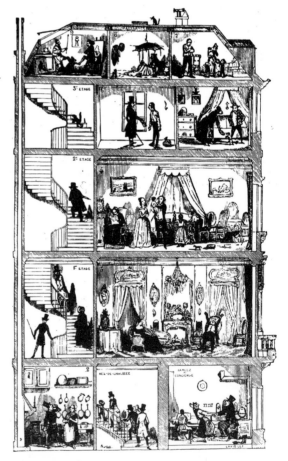

68 Cartoonist's interior of the standard apartment house chosen by Haussmann to line the new boulevards. Hundreds of these dwellings were erected, and the uniformity of their façades provoked widespread protest. The design clearly reflects a society in which wealth is unequally distributed

Of the great public works of the Second Empire the most
spectacular was the reconstruction of Paris. In 1853 Baron
Haussmann was appointed Prefect of the Seine Department,
and on the day that he was installed in office Napoleon III
showed him a plan of Paris on which various projects for the
improvement of the city were marked. For seventeen years
Emperor and Prefect worked closely together on their grand
design to make the capital of France the most modern and
beautiful city in Europe. The plan was carried out in three
phases. The main features of the 'first network' of roads,
planned for the most part before Napoleon III's accession,
were the extension of the Rue de Rivoli, the completion of
the Louvre and the wholesale-food market, and the replan-
ning of the Bois de Boulogne. These works, carried out by

81

direct municipal labour, were virtually completed by 1858, the cost (272 million francs) being shared by the State and the city of Paris. The 'second network', which cost nearly 412 million francs, was planned in 1858 when the government and the municipal authorities came to an agreement by which the State contributed one-third of the cost up to a maximum of 50 million francs. The 'third network' was constructed at the same time as the second but without financial aid from the government. These two networks included the completion of a great highway through Paris from Neuilly in the east by way of the Étoile to Vincennes in the west; the construction of new approaches to the main railway stations; the provision of links between recently built industrial suburbs and the city centre; and the construction of a ring road and of spacious squares, such as the Étoile, at the meeting-point of several boulevards. Haussmann was also responsible for providing Paris with a new water supply and a new system of sewers. The water came from two streams in Burgundy and was collected at the Belleville Reservoir. A second scheme brought water from the Vanne (a tributary of the Yonne) to Paris. The sewage was carried in a huge collector from the Place de la Concorde to the River Seine at Asnières.

The methods that Haussmann used to pay for the rebuilding of Paris – particularly the third network, which received no State subsidy – eventually led to his fall from office. He used the annual surplus of the 'ordinary' municipal budget to finance loans to cover the growing deficit of the 'extraordinary' budget. He called this 'productive spending' and argued that borrowing to pay for public works was perfectly justified since municipal improvements ultimately produced increased revenues from the rates.

Haussmann's rebuilding of Paris encouraged provincial cities to follow the example of the capital. The city fathers of Lyons, Marseilles, Le Havre and other towns hastened to borrow money from the Crédit Foncier to build or to reconstruct highways, bridges, markets, town halls, parks and other municipal amenities. These public works, like the construction of railways, stimulated employment in the building industry and in those branches of manufacture which supplied building contractors with the materials and goods they required.

In pursuing a policy of constructing railways and public works, the Emperor was following in the footsteps of the first Napoleon who had built great military roads and had spent large sums on the improvement of his capital. But Napoleon III's fiscal policy was very different from that of his uncle. Under Napoleon I, French farmers and manufacturers had been completely protected from foreign competition. This policy had survived Waterloo, though in a somewhat milder form, and with the coming of the Second Empire the home market was still protected by import prohibitions and high tariffs. The French were accustomed to protection and the views of free traders like Bastiat and Chevalier made little headway. Napoleon III was no doctrinaire free trader, but he did believe that in the long run the removal of import prohibitions and a substantial reduction of import duties would stimulate the French economy. He saw that high protection shielded manufacturers from foreign competition and provided them with little incentive to introduce improved machinery or modern business methods.

Napoleon III had to proceed cautiously in seeking to reform the fiscal system. In 1856 an attempt to replace certain prohibitions by import duties met with such vigorous opposition that the plan was withdrawn from the legislature. A way out of the difficulty was for the Emperor to reform the tariff by embodying the reductions in import duties in a commercial treaty with a foreign country. Under the constitution he was authorized to sign and to ratify trade agreements without submitting them to the Chamber for approval. This method was adopted by Napoleon III in January 1860. The French government signed a commercial treaty with Britain – on the basis of a draft negotiated in secret by Richard Cobden and Michel Chevalier – by which the maximum rate of French import duties on British goods was fixed at 30 per cent for four years and at 25 per cent afterwards. Many of the actual French import duties – fixed by conventions signed in the autumn of 1860 – were much lower than the maximum rates. In return Gladstone, in his Budget of 1860, removed all duties on French manufactures (such as silks) and reduced British duties on French wines and spirits. France signed similar commercial treaties with Belgium, Italy and Prussia (on behalf of the German customs union) and in this way a low-tariff *bloc* was established in western Europe within which trade flowed much more freely than before. The gloomy predictions of the protectionists that the new fiscal policy would lead to economic disaster were not fulfilled and Napoleon III tried to sugar the pill of the unpopular Cobden-Chevalier Treaty by granting industrialists a State loan of 40 million francs to enable them to buy new machines and expand their plants. The stimulus of foreign competition brought about by the low-tariff commercial agreements was one of the factors that in the 1860s contributed to the modernization of several French industries, such as textiles, iron and steel.

The government of the Second Empire was closely concerned with the creation of two important banks which fostered the economic development of the country: the Crédit Foncier and the Crédit Mobilier. The Crédit Foncier, established by a decree published in 1852, was a bank which was granted a monopoly of land-mortgage business, and enjoyed a State subsidy of 10 million francs. Two years later it became a semi-State institution, since its Governor and his two Deputies were thenceforth to be appointed by the Emperor. It began as a bank which lent money to landowners on the security of their estates, but developed virtually into an institution which financed municipal public works.

The Crédit Mobilier was a relatively new kind of credit bank of industry. In 1852 its constitution received government approval, and it was required to submit regular reports of its transactions to the Minister of the Interior. At the height of its career the Crédit Mobilier handled nearly one-third of the new shares launched on the Paris Exchange; it promoted a number of important enterprises including several consolidated railways, the gasworks of Paris and Marseilles, the Transatlantic Maritime Company and a firm which played an important part in the rebuilding of Paris; it also made substantial investments in relatively underdeveloped countries, such as Spain and the Habsburg dominions.

Ever since the days of Peter the Great the Tsars of Russia had tried to bribe and cajole landowners and merchants to take a greater interest in promoting the industrial development of the country, but only a limited measure of success had attended their efforts. Many nobles regarded industrial activities as an undignified occupation and merchants were deterred from establishing factories by the shortage of labour and the bureaucratic supervision of economic affairs. Initially, therefore, it was the foreign capitalist, entrepreneur and skilled worker who played the leading role in setting up large modern manufacturing establishments in Russia. The introduction of mechanical cotton-spinning, for example, was due largely to the German entrepreneur Ludwig Knoop.

Though born in Bremen, Knoop had worked as a young man in the offices of the Manchester firm of C. B. Jersey. At the age of eighteen he went to Russia to assist his firm's representative in Moscow. Before long he had set up a modern cotton spinning-mill at Nikolskoye (near Moscow) for the firm of Morozov. Altogether he established 122 cotton factories in Russia, working in close association with a small group of Lancashire firms: C. B. Jersey of Manchester, Platt Brothers of Oldham, Hick, Hargreaves & Co. of Bolton, and Mather & Platt of Salford.

The founding of a modern iron industry in the Ukraine owed much to the Welsh ironmaster John Hughes, who had previously been manager at the works of the Millwall Iron &

70 Count Sergei
Witte (1849–1915),
promoter of industry,
Russian Minister of
Finance in the closing
years of the last
century

Shipbuilding Co. in London. In 1869 his New Russia Company
received very favourable financial inducements from the
Russian government to set up an ironworks in the Donetz
valley to make rails for the new railways. The first furnace
was fired in 1872, and twenty years later a town had grown up
round the plant, by then employing about 6,000 men.

The rise of Russia's great oil industry was due largely to the
initiative of the Swedish brothers Robert and Ludvig Nobel.
In the 1870s they set up a company to sink oil-wells at Baku,
and to establish oil-refineries. Their tanker *Zoroaster* (built in
1878 by the Lindholmen-Motala shipbuilding yard in Sweden)
could carry 250 tons of kerosene in 21 iron cylinders. In the

71 The 4,000-mile Trans-Siberian railway was probably Witte's greatest
achievement. Right, a scene a few years after the line's completion in 1904 ▶

1880s the Nobels' tankers carried oil in holds lined with cement. They sailed regularly on the Caspian Sea from Baku to Astrakhan, whence the oil was sent up the Volga in the Nobels' specially constructed barges.

Foreigners also helped to build Russia's early railway lines. Much of the capital of the Great Russia Railway Company of 1857 was raised abroad. Three French banks were particularly active in providing money for the company and the necessary bridges, locomotives and rolling-stock were largely supplied by French firms.

However, Russia's industrial progress in the 1890s was to a great extent the achievement of Count Sergei Witte, Minister of Finance between 1892 and 1903. In the eleven years that he held office Witte pressed forward energetically with his plans to speed up the pace of industrialization. Since he considered the construction of a greatly improved railway system the key to future economic progress, he had the railways of Russia nearly doubled in length: Moscow was linked with the ports of Archangel and Riga and the textile centre of Ivanovo-Vognesensk; St Petersburg gained direct access to the Ukraine, while Kiev was joined to the Donetz valley, and Rostov, on the Don, was linked with the oilfield of Baku. Witte's most spectacular railway was the Trans-Siberian line, of which well over 3,000 miles had been completed by 1899. Heavy government investment in railways fostered the expansion of the iron, steel and engineering industries; there was great activity in the Krivoi-Rog ironfield, the Donetz coal basin and the Baku oilfield; the industrial resources of Siberia and Central Asia

began to be opened up, and even the remote Chinese provinces of Manchuria and Korea were subject to Russian economic penetration.

To finance an enormous programme of public works Witte relied heavily upon government borrowing from abroad and upon persuading foreign capitalists to invest in Russian industrial enterprises. In answer to his critics Witte insisted that in the past all underdeveloped countries had relied upon borrowed money to assist in financing the early phase of industrialization. But his financial policy undoubtedly placed heavy burdens upon the Russian taxpayers and consumers. Witte's critics complained that prices were rising, that grain was being exported even when there was a poor harvest, and that 'Witte's system' could survive only so long as foreign – particularly French – investors were prepared to go on buying Russian State bonds and shares in new Russian joint-stock companies. They claimed that many of the new industries were being run by foreign entrepreneurs for the benefit of foreign investors, and that although some manufacturing regions (such as the Donetz valley) might appear to be flourishing, older industrial areas (such as the Urals) were declining. The critics also argued that if industry were to flourish there must be a heavy home demand for consumer goods.

Towards the end of his term of office Witte began to realize the need for overall State economic planning. With incomparable energy he extended his influence over the activities of one branch of the civil service after another. But in the Russia of his day he could never hope to gain decisive control over all aspects of economic life. Moreover, he came to see that the peasant problem lay at the root of Russia's difficulties in the 1890s. His recommendations for dealing with it fell upon deaf ears, though they foreshadowed the subsequent agrarian reforms of Stolypin. While Witte believed that an autocratic form of government was essential for Russia, he realized that Nicholas II lacked the understanding and will-power needed to carry out the crucial reforms.

The efforts of European governments to stimulate economic growth during the Industrial Revolution might have achieved only a very limited success had not private enterprise been prepared to play its part in building up new enterprises. Among the many thousands of pioneer entrepreneurs who helped to transform Europe from an agrarian into a predominantly manufacturing region were inventors, skilled craftsmen merchants, landed gentry, financiers and even serfs.

INVENTOR-ENTREPRENEUR WERNER SIEMENS

Werner Siemens (1816–92) was a famous German inventor–entrepreneur. His father could not afford to give him a university education, but as a cadet in the Prussian Artillery, he received a sound technical education at the United Engineering and Artillery School in Berlin (1835–8). In 1842, having secured a patent for galvanic gilding and plating, he came to an agreement with a silversmith named Henniger to exploit the process commercially, and sold the English patent rights to the Birmingham firm of Elkington, for £1,500. Siemens next engaged in various experiments connected with electric telegraphy, and in 1846 he successfully used rubber to insulate electrified wires on the Berlin-Anhalt Railway. In 1847, with the financial assistance of his cousin Georg Siemens, he went into partnership with the mechanic J. G. Halske to set up a telegraph factory.

In 1848 Siemens served in Prussia's newly created Ministry of Commerce which was engaged in the urgent task of laying an underground electric telegraph between Berlin and Frankfurt am Main. This line – the first long telegraph line in Europe – was completed early in 1849. Siemens's next assignment was to supervise the construction of an underground telegraph line from Berlin to Cologne, Aachen, and Verviers where it was linked to the overhead line to Brussels. His first telegraph lines, however, soon failed to function satisfactorily. Believing that this was due to the refusal of the officials of the Ministry of Commerce to follow his advice, he wrote a pamphlet expressing his views on the matter. The result was a breach with the Prussian bureaucracy, and for many years Siemens and Halske received no orders from the railway administration. This forced the firm to deal only with private railway companies in Prussia and elsewhere. By 1849 Siemens and Halske had already supplied the Russian government with apparatus for the St Petersburg-Moscow telegraph line. And in 1851 the company's reputation was enhanced by the award of a Council Medal at the International Exhibition held in London. In 1852 Siemens paid two visits to Russia and his firm secured orders to link Riga and Bolderaja, and St Petersburg and Kronstadt by telegraph. In the following year Siemens was entrusted with the construction of the railway telegraph from Warsaw to the Prussian frontier and this was accomplished with the assistance of his brother Carl. After the Crimean War, during which the firm had laid the St Petersburg-Warsaw telegraph, there followed a spate of further orders. Carl Siemens was placed in charge of a subsidiary firm at St Petersburg and was responsible for carrying out the many orders received from the Russian government. In 1858 the managing and maintaining of the Russian telegraphs alone earned 80,000 roubles a year.

While the Russian subsidiary of Siemens and Halske was covering the Tsar's dominions with a network of telegraphs in the 1850s, the Berlin firm supplied Newall & Co. with the electrical apparatus for the Cagliari-Bône (Sardinia-Algeria) cable and the Suez-Karachi cable. In 1859 the London branch of the firm, run by Werner's brother, William, was entrusted by the British government with the task of preparing and testing future submarine cables. And in 1860 Werner and William Siemens described their methods in a paper read to the British Association, and William Siemens established a new plant near Woolwich to cope with orders for cables. At first the cable side of the business was run at a loss and Halske began to complain. So Werner and Carl set up an independent company in England called Siemens Brothers.

72, 73 Inventor-entrepreneur Werner Siemens (1816–92) and the dynamo he invented in 1866

In the 1860s the Siemens firms in Berlin, London and St Petersburg set up a new Anglo-German company to construct the Indo-European telegraph line from London to Calcutta, which followed an overland route through Russia and Persia but used a submarine cable in the Black Sea. At about the same time a branch of the St Petersburg firm of Siemens constructed several telegraph lines for the Russian government in the Caucasus. When the lines were completed, a fourth Siemens brother, Walter, with financial aid from Werner and William, set up a copper-mine in the Caucasus. Meanwhile, the London company added to its reputation by successfully testing the Malta-Alexandria cable; its business grew to such an extent that by 1874 it was operating its own cable-laying ship, the *Faraday*.

Despite his numerous business interests Werner Siemens continued his experimental work and devised numerous electrical appliances in the 1850s and 1860s. The dynamo, his greatest achievement – invented in 1866, when he was sixty years old – was described in a communication to the Berlin Academy of Sciences on 17 January 1867. A month later his brother William exhibited a dynamo to the Royal Society in England, and one of the first large dynamos to be built by

91

Siemens and Halske was shown at the Paris Exhibition of 1867. In his later years Siemens was actively concerned with the application of electric power to new purposes: to locomotives and trams, to lifts and street lighting. In 1880 his first electric lift was in use at the industrial exhibition at Mannheim; in 1881 the first electric tram ran in Berlin, and in the following year the Potsdamer Platz in Berlin was lit with arc-lamps. In Berlin in the same year Siemens and Halske established a plant for making filament lamps.

The climax of Werner Siemens's career as an entrepreneur came in 1883 when his firm concluded an agreement with its newly founded rival, Emil Rathenau's German Edison Company: a few years later the two firms established the great German electrical cartel called the Allgemeine Elektrizitäts-Gesellschaft (A.E.G.). Siemens retired from business in 1890 and died two years later. The publication of most of his numerous technical papers in 1889–91 showed that his contribution to science and technology and his career as a captain of industry were equally distinguished.

74 The Siemens-owned *Faraday*, designed to lay submarine cables, abuilding

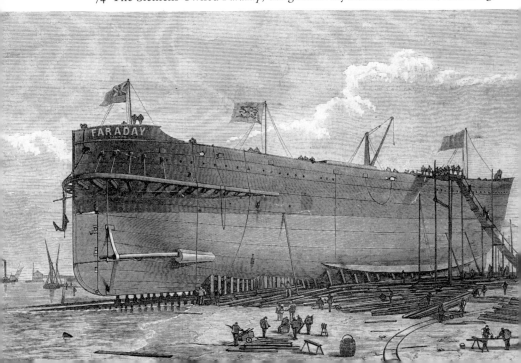

75 The Siemens electric tram at the Paris Electrical Exhibition of 1881

Merchant-entrepreneurs were familiar figures in the early industrial age. The transition from household to factory production was largely carried out by merchants who extended their interests from dealing in commodities to their manufacture. Sometimes merchants began by financing and organizing the work of village craftsmen, thereafter establishing factories with power-driven machinery to manufacture goods formerly made by domestic workers. John Marshall, one of the leading textile manufacturers in Leeds in the early nineteenth century, was an entrepreneur of this type. Marshall's father, Jeremiah, a draper in Leeds dealing in Irish linens, had been a successful businessman and accumulated a modest fortune. When he died suddenly in 1787 his twenty-two-year-old son John decided to enlarge the family business by developing an interest in the spinning and weaving of flax.

93

A patent for the mechanical spinning of flax had recently been taken out by Kendrew and Porthouse, and Marshall hoped to emulate in the linen industry what Arkwright and others had achieved in the cotton industry. In 1788, in partnership with Samuel Fenton and Ralph Dearlove, he leased a newly built watermill near Leeds. At first he had little success with either the Kendrew-Porthouse spinning machine or the Cartwright power-loom, which he also tried. Fortunately, he was able to secure the services of Matthew Murray, a young mechanic who later established his reputation as one of England's leading engineers and machine-builders. Murray's improvements to the Kendrew-Porthouse spinning machine and his invention of a satisfactory flax-carding machine paved the way for the future success of Marshall's firm. In 1791 Marshall sold his drapery business, borrowed money from relatives and friends, and moved to larger premises in Water Lane, which lay between Leeds and Holbeck.

76, 77 Two famous spinning machines of the eighteenth century. Far left, the Spinning Jenny, invented by a Blackburn carpenter, James Hargreaves, *c.* 1764, enabling a single spinner to spin many threads simultaneously. Left, Arkwright's twist frame, patented in 1769, the first self-acting machine to spin threads sufficiently fine and hard for a weaver to use as the cloth warp

78 Sir Richard Arkwright (1732–92), inventor and entrepreneur, dominant figure in British textiles at the outset of John Marshall's career

79 Interior of an English cotton mill, 1862. Driving belts link several machines to an overhead shaft powered by a single steam engine

Soon after the new mill was opened, the commercial crisis of 1793 – brought about by the outbreak of war with France – caught Marshall unawares. But he quickly took advantage of the situation to dissolve his partnership with Fenton and Dearlove – who lost the money that they had invested – and so secured complete control over the firm. Despite his losses he was able to raise new loans and to take advantage of the drop in yarn imports from the Continent during the war to expand his business. He concentrated upon spinning by machinery, and gave out the yarn to domestic hand-loom weavers. In December 1793 two Shrewsbury woollen merchants, the brothers Thomas and Benjamin Benyon, became Marshall's new partners, providing new capital in return for half of the profits. The firm now expanded rapidly. A second mill with 1,200 spindles, operated by a 28-h.p. Boulton and Watt steam engine, was opened in 1795, but burned down within five months. While it was being rebuilt, Marshall set up a bleach-yard at Wortley.

By 1803 Marshall and his partners, with 7,000 spindles and 1,000 operatives, were running by far the largest linen manufactory in England. But the partnership failed to work satisfactorily, since both Marshall and the Benyon brothers sought complete control over the firm. Eventually, in 1805, Marshall was able to buy out the Benyons and assume control of the Leeds mill himself. The new arrangement worked well and in the ten years 1805–15 Marshall made his fortune as a flax-spinner. In his history of the firm W. G. Rimmer observes that during the Napoleonic Wars 'the fall in yarn imports meant that the total supply from home and overseas sources contracted more sharply than demand and higher flax prices could be passed on to the consumer. . . . The profit on yarn rose from 2s a bundle in the 1790s to at least 4s after 1803.'

By 1815 Marshall was the acknowledged leader of the English linen industry. When the Swiss metallurgist J. C. Fischer looked over Marshall's factory in 1814 he particularly admired the heckling and fibre-sorting machines, although Marshall

80 Josiah Wedgwood (1730–95), Staffordshire potter and entrepreneur, another great pioneer of the Industrial Revolution. His significance consists, above all, in his scientific approach to the materials of pottery manufacture, to the deployment of labour, and to the needs of an industrial community

reminded his visitor that the mechanical spinning of flax had not yet reached the standard achieved in the spinning of cotton by machinery. After the Napoleonic Wars Marshall left the day-to-day running of the mills to younger men, spending less time in the factory and more in establishing himself as a public figure in the West Riding, and as a country gentleman in the Lake District. But in a crisis Marshall's influence remained decisive. In the late 1820s he was quick to appreciate the significance of a new invention – a machine for the wet spinning of fine linen yarn – and the prosperity of the firm in the 1830s was very largely due to his foresight in introducing this machine in his mills. Marshall's success as a pioneer entrepreneur may be explained by his skill in purchasing raw materials, by his readiness to adopt new spinning machinery and new dyeing processes, by the energetic manner in which he searched for new markets and by the highly efficient manner with which he organized the running of his mills.

97

Many pioneer entrepreneurs were craftsmen who turned small domestic workshops into large industrial undertakings. Such an industrialist was Alfred Krupp. The Krupp family had long been respected merchants in Essen, but as a young man Friedrich Krupp – Alfred's father – became interested in the metal industry after working in his grandmother's foundry (the Gutehoffnunghütte) at Sterkrade. When his grandmother sold these ironworks Friedrich Krupp converted a fulling-mill into a foundry and went into partnership first with the von Kechel brothers and later with Nicolai. The partners claimed to be able to make a crucible cast steel similar to that produced in Sheffield by the Huntsman process, and Krupp, a member of the town council, therefore felt free to give much of his time to public duties, and neglected his foundry. But his partners were not the experts they made themselves out to be. In 1817 Krupp decided to devote himself entirely to his ironworks, and produced samples of cast steel of such high quality that the Prussian Mint promised him a contract provided regular supplies of high-quality steel could be guaranteed. Instead of continuing his experiments, Krupp now sank the rest of his capital into the construction of new ironworks which were opened in October 1819. Although the new plant frequently produced samples of steel that fully met the requirements of various German mints Krupp was never able to send these mints regular supplies of steel dies of high quality. He died in 1826 after a long illness, at the age of thirty-nine.

Krupp's wife inherited the steelworks and his eldest son, Alfred, although only fourteen years old, became its new manager. Alfred Krupp was no novice: from his father he had learned 'the secret process of the preparation of cast steel', and during his father's illness had bought the raw materials and run the plant himself. He was determined to revive the fortunes of the ironworks which then employed only seven men. Realizing that crucible cast steel of the best quality could be made only from high-grade iron bars, he decided in future to purchase all his raw material from the Osmund furnaces of the Brüninghaus brothers at Versetal. In each of the first two years during which he managed the plant he produced less than three tons of cast steel, some of which was sold in the form of rolls, while some was made into coin-dies, tools and small machine parts.

Krupp extended his knowledge of the metalworking industries by visiting numerous hammerworks, wireworks, brass manufactories and cutlery workshops in the districts of Berg and Mark. It occurred to him that some of the tools he saw in use could be improved if they were made of steel, and from time to time he secured small orders for his steel on his travels. Four years after his father's death he opened an additional workshop, backed by his uncle, Carl Schulz, and other relations, but his new machines for turning and polishing were home-made and crude. Krupp later recalled that in those early days he himself 'acted as clerk, letter-writer, cashier, smith, smelter, coke-pounder, nightwatchman at the converting furnace, and took on many other jobs as well.'

In 1832, when the teething troubles of the new plant appeared to have been surmounted, Krupp embarked upon a series of journeys in Germany and abroad to drum up new business and inspect such steelworks as would admit him. He went first to southern Germany, where he secured numerous orders from goldsmiths and silversmiths. Upon the founding of the Zollverein in 1834, Krupp visited the south-German States, Saxony and finally Berlin, where he did good business with Vollgold and Son, a leading firm of silversmiths.

Krupp now felt justified in expanding his works and in turning from water-power to steam. In 1835, his cousin Fritz von Müller became his partner, investing 10,000 Thalers in the firm, and a 20-h.p. engine, built at the Gutehoffnung foundry, was installed. The plant was still a small one – employing between forty and fifty men – but the high quality of the steel which it produced firmly established its reputation. Krupp's works at Essen began to attract distinguished visitors, such as Friedrich Harkort (a pioneer industrialist in the Ruhr)

81, 82 Cartoon of a man whose name is synonymous with German steel and German guns: Alfred Krupp (1812–87), a towering figure in his prime. Opposite, the modest steelworks at Essen whose management Alfred was to assume at the age of fourteen, on the death of his father

and Ernst von Bodelschwingh (the President of the Rhineland province).

In 1838–9 Krupp left Essen on a fifteen-month tour of France and England. He spent several months in Paris showing samples of his steel to hundreds of goldsmiths. In England, where his old school-friend Fritz Sölling provided him with letters of introduction, Krupp used the name 'Schropp' in the hope of hiding his identity from the owners of the steelworks and engineering plants he visited. In January 1839, when he was in Liverpool, he boasted of his success in deceiving the English. He wrote: 'Only yesterday at a place five miles away, where I had gone for a walk with Fritz Sölling, I saw, without any introduction, a new rolling mill for copper plates, which has only been working for a short time and where no one is admitted. I was properly booted and spurred and the proprietor was flattered that a couple of such good fellows should deign to inspect his works.'

Krupp's visit to England was cut short by an urgent letter from his brother Hermann concerning the financial difficulties of the firm. The works in the old fulling-mill had been sold in May 1839 but even this did not provide all the money that was needed. On his return to Essen, Krupp appears to have taken the

83 Part of the Krupp steel complex at Essen, 1880 ▶

view that the only solution to his financial problems was to continue his travels in search of fresh orders. Between December 1839 and the summer of 1843 he was seldom at the steelworks: a visit to Berlin secured an order for a silver-rolling mill from Vollgold and Son; in Vienna he obtained an order from the Mint, but there were exasperating delays in securing payment; in May 1843 he supplied a factory near Vienna with machinery he had himself invented for the mass-production of spoons and forks.

In 1844 the partnership between Krupp and Müller was dissolved, as Krupp was unwilling to allow his cousin to risk any more money in the enterprise. Once more Krupp was able to find a partner who had adequate capital to invest in the firm – his friend Fritz Sölling.

In the 1840s, true to his policy of continually seeking new outlets for steel, Krupp began to experiment with armaments, but the Prussian government showed no immediate interest in his new steel helmets or his rifle and cannon barrels. A brief boom was followed by a slump in 1847 and a revolution in 1848. Krupp was so short of cash in 1848 that he had to melt down the family silver to raise funds to pay his men's wages. Fortunately, an order from St Petersburg for rolling-mill machinery to make spoons and forks was received shortly afterwards. The following year there was a further improvement in Krupp's prospects, for he secured a large order from the Cologne-Minden Railway for steel springs and axles.

Railway materials now became a significant part of the firm's output. In the bitterly cold winter of 1850 Krupp travelled all over northern Germany to show samples of his steel to various railway administrations. Large quantities of steel were required for the new railway orders, and Krupp found that it was now too expensive to use iron from the Osmund furnaces. With some regret he introduced a puddling-furnace in his own plant. When the Great Exhibition was held in London in 1851 Krupp – showing a six-pounder (with a cast-steel barrel), axles for railway coaches, and a 2,150-

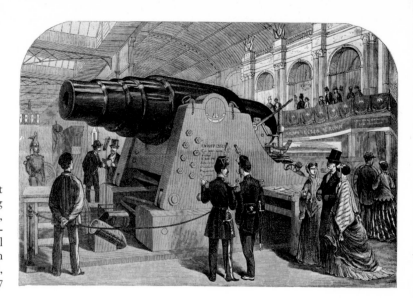

84 A present
for the King
of Prussia,
Krupp's fifty-
ton steel
cannon on
show in Paris,
1867

kilogramme block of crucible cast steel, the largest that had ever been made – attracted considerable attention and he was awarded a bronze Council medal.

In the 1850s Krupp's enterprise flourished as never before. There was a great boom in the Ruhr at this time: local coal-mines and ironworks expanded with astonishing rapidity, and the commercial crisis of 1857 proved to be only a temporary interruption. When he returned to Essen after the Great Exhibition Krupp installed an enormous steam hammer at his works. At the same time he successfully completed his experiments in producing weldless, cast-steel railway tyres. These tyres became an important Krupp product, and three interlocking rings representing three railway tyres became the Krupp trademark. In 1855 a special plant for the manufacture of tyres was opened and within ten years an annual output of 20,000 tyres had been achieved. At the industrial exhibitions in Munich (1854) and Paris (1855) Krupp showed further blocks of steel, railway tyres and gun-barrels and secured many new orders. In 1857 he at last obtained, from Egypt, a small order for his guns with cast-steel barrels; then in 1859 the Prussian government placed an order for 300 steel barrels.

103

85 Overleaf, 'Fritz'—a colossal steam hammer
installed by Krupp at Essen in 1861 ▶

The firm continued to expand in the 1860s: a contract of 1863 to supply the Russian government with steel guns was the largest order that Krupp had ever received; it was followed by many orders for armaments from foreign governments, and the co-operation of Russian gunnery experts and Krupp's engineers led to improvements in the construction of steel barrels. Once more Krupp extended his plant and by 1864 he was employing 6,000 men. Soon after 1856, when a new method of making steel was invented by Sir Henry Bessemer, it became clear that steel, for so long an expensive metal produced only in small quantities, could be made at a competitive price and on a much larger scale than before. Fortunately, Alfred Longsdon, Krupp's representative in London, was able, through his brother Frederick, a close friend of Bessemer, to secure the right to make the new steel under licence. Krupp could now add steel rails to his other railway products.

When Germany was united in 1871 the firm of Krupp had become a mammoth, many-sided concern. Krupp owned iron-ore deposits and had leased a coal-mine. He could make his own bar iron and could turn out a great variety of steel goods. The most important products of the Krupp steelworks were armaments, railway equipment and ship-yard materials.

86 *Panthéon du Comic-Finance.*
Detail of a nineteenth-century cartoon presenting the caricatures of leading figures in French commerce and industry

The financier-entrepreneurs were men of a very different type from the industrial pioneers who were inventors, craftsmen or merchants. The financiers were bankers, accountants, and dealers in stocks and shares who were at home in the boardroom rather than on the shop floor. Rarely possessing any technical training, they relied upon the services of managers, engineers and other experts to run enterprises they founded. The skill of the financier lay in appreciating the possibility of developing a particular industry or public utility, in raising the necessary capital from banks or other investors, and in founding a company to run the enterprise.

The Pereire brothers were Jews born in Bordeaux – Emile in 1800 and Isaac six years later. Religious intolerance in Portugal had led a number of Portuguese Jews to settle in Bordeaux in the early eighteenth century. They were not persecuted in France, but could not enjoy full rights of citizenship. Finance, however, was an occupation open to them, and the Pereire family ran a private bank. Emile came to Paris as a young man in 1822 and worked on the Stock Exchange, while Isaac, who joined him there, soon became chief accountant of the firm of Vital-Reux. Through their cousin, Olindes Rodrigues, they came to meet the philosopher Saint-Simon.

At this time the doctrines of Saint-Simon had attracted the support of some of the most progressive young intellectuals in the country. Saint-Simon argued that after the storms of the Revolution and the Napoleonic era the country should not be allowed to sink into the lethargy of a reaction inspired by

the ideas of the *ancien régime*. He condemned what he called
the 'feudal' and the 'military' organization of society and
denounced the survival of the nobility and the idle rich.
He proposed the establishment of a nationally planned industrial society which would promote the well-being of the
peasants, the craftsmen and the industrial workers. He argued
that secular affairs should be controlled by industrialists and
bankers, and that moral affairs should be directed by men of
science. He advocated the promotion of industrial growth by a
great programme of public works. In 1814 he put forward a
plan for a federated Europe, and his followers became leading
advocates of free trade and world peace.

Saint-Simon's ideas were summarized in lectures delivered
by his disciples after his death. In some respects the disciples
went further than their master, particularly in their advocacy
of a new banking system. The Saint-Simonians suggested that
each major industry should have its credit bank which would
link investors, who had money to spare, with manufacturers,
who required capital to expand their businesses. These credit

87, 88 The brothers Emile and Isaac Pereire, banker-entrepreneurs, railway pioneers, and co-founders of the Crédit Mobilier through which they were able to mobilize private capital for the development of French industry

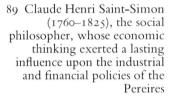

89 Claude Henri Saint-Simon (1760–1825), the social philosopher, whose economic thinking exerted a lasting influence upon the industrial and financial policies of the Pereires

finance houses would come under the control of the central bank. The ideas of Saint-Simon – and of his leading disciples – had a profound influence long after his death. His teachings inspired two different movements: Utopian socialism on the one hand, finance-capitalism on the other. Hayek observes that the real significance of Saint-Simonianism lay less in fostering socialist ideas, than in the promotion of 'finance-capitalism growing up through the intimate connection between banking and industry'. It was this second aspect of Saint-Simon's doctrines that was all important as far as the Pereire brothers were concerned.

After Saint-Simon had quarrelled with his two leading followers – the historian Thierry and the positivist Comte – he was fortunate in finding a patron in Olindes Rodrigues. In the two remaining years of his life – he died in 1825 – Saint-Simon secured the support of a new group of disciples, largely composed of young Jewish intellectuals. While Isaac Pereire was an enthusiastic convert, Emile had little interest in the religious side of the movement, but grasped the significance

109

of its main economic doctrines. Early in the 1830s, when the eccentric Prosper Enfantin tried to develop Saint-Simon's thought into a mystical religion, Rodrigues and the Pereires left the movement. But for the rest of their lives they continued to be influenced by Saint-Simon's economic teachings. They believed that public utilities and industrial enterprises should be founded to further social ideals, and not merely to make money. They accepted the view that economic growth could best be fostered by the establishment of a sound system of credit operated by the banks. They believed that it was man's destiny to gain an increasing mastery over the forces of nature and that the promotion of industrial expansion could be achieved by making full use of all available scientific and technical knowledge. In this way there would be a steady improvement in the living standards of all classes in society.

During their association with the Saint-Simonians the Pereires established a reputation for themselves as journalists. They supported the Saint-Simonian cause in articles which appeared in the *Producteur*, the *Organisateur*, the *Globe* and various other periodicals. During the financial crisis of 1830 they collaborated to produce a memorandum which suggested that a credit bank should be established to lend money to industry. Its directors would be bankers, merchants and manufacturers, and its capital consist of 50 million francs contributed by the State, supplemented by the issue of interest-bearing banknotes. In this *Project de Banque* can be seen the germ of the idea that later culminated in their founding of a new institution, the Crédit Mobilier.

In 1832 the Pereires, endeavouring to put some of Saint-Simon's ideas into practice, soon discovered that this was possible only in association with the leading bankers of Paris. Saint-Simon had stressed the need to improve communications, and the Pereires, realizing that a national system of French railways must be centred upon the capital, proposed to make a start by constructing a line from Paris to Saint-Germain. Emile Pereire submitted a plan for this railway to the

90 Paris street scene in the 1870s. In the background is the Gare de l'Est, terminal of the Eastern Railway built at the instigation of James Rothschild

Department of Highways and Bridges in September 1832, but it was not until July 1835 that the government passed a law authorizing the construction of the line – Thiers dismissing the project with the remark: 'We must give the Parisians this as a toy, but it will never carry a passenger or a parcel.'

In November 1835 Emile Pereire formed a railway company with the aid of the Rothschild, Eichthal, Thurneyssen and Davillier banks. Each bank put up 1,175,000 francs, while Emile Pereire himself invested 300,000 francs, and in August 1837 the Paris-Saint-Germain line – the first French railway built solely for passenger traffic – was opened to Le Pecq. However, the second railway built by the Pereires was less successful. This was the Paris-Versailles line, opened in 1840, running on the right bank of the Seine, which after two years found itself in competition with a similar line built on the left bank. The construction of the two lines appears to have reflected not the rivalry of banking-houses of Rothschilds and

111

91 The railway disaster. Above, a real danger in the infancy of locomotive design: a boiler explodes on the Leipzig–Dresden line, 1846

Foulds, but the rivalry of those districts of Paris and Versailles served by the two lines. In May 1842, however, the left-bank line was the scene of a disaster in which forty-five lives were lost. For a time people were reluctant to travel on the Paris lines, and neither made a profit. 'These losses have so alarmed and prejudiced the public,' 'that the building of railways in France has been delayed for several years.' The disputes between the rival lines to Versailles took some time to settle. Amalgamation of the two companies was the obvious solution, but by the time of the Revolution of 1848, this had still not been agreed.

The Pereires next turned their attention to the construction of a much more important railway than the small suburban lines from Paris to Saint-Germain and Versailles. This was the Northern line which ran from Paris to Amiens, Lille and the Channel ports and was also connected with the Belgian railway

92 Many Europeans greeted the advent of railways with bitter indignation, others with alarm and foreboding. The often high-handed expropriation of land to accommodate the proliferating networks, fatal railway accidents, and fires caused by live coals discharged by locomotives aroused widespread resentment. Right, a typical cartoon of the time depicts yet more unwilling victims of the railway juggernaut

93, 94 Below, two cartoons betraying public misgivings about railway safety. Left, an undertaker takes a keen interest in a prospective passenger. Right, the suggested method of insuring against accidents: 'Tie a couple of directors *à la mazeppa* to every engine that starts with a train'

HOW TO INSURE AGAINST RAILWAY ACCIDENTS.

system, thus linking the French capital with the coal and iron industries of the Nord Department and the textile industries of Lille and Roubaix. It also provided the quickest route between Paris and the capitals of England and Belgium. Emile Pereire played an important part in the negotiations which culminated in August 1845 in the amalgamation of rival companies which had been formed. The Northern Railway was opened on 17 June 1846 and proved to be a profitable venture for the investors. The Pereires were also involved in the construction of the Paris–Lyons Railway.

In the 1850s and 1860s, during the Second Empire, the Pereires greatly extended their business activities. Before 1848 they had raised money for their railway enterprises from James Rothschild and other French – and English – bankers. Later they financed their numerous ventures in quite a different way, by founding a relatively new kind of bank – the Crédit Mobilier – through which they could obtain funds directly from the investing public. Since it could issue shares in new companies, the new bank had access to a vast source of capital which had hitherto been almost untapped. But in the end the Pereires paid the price for challenging the old monopoly of the great Paris banks. They earned the enmity of their former ally James Rothschild, whose hands were tied at first since – as an Orleanist – he was regarded by Louis Napoleon with some suspicion. Rothschild's warnings to the Emperor concerning the Crédit Mobilier met with no response. But the opposition of the Rothschilds not only held up some of the most promising of the Pereires' projects but was also a decisive factor in their downfall in 1867.

Louis Napoleon, to whom Sainte-Beuve once referred as 'Saint-Simon on horseback', gave his blessing to the Crédit Mobilier, and the Pereires suceeded in setting up not only their credit bank but also numerous public utilities at home and abroad. Their Maritime Transatlantic Company (1861) established a steamship service to the United States, the West Indies and Mexico. Their Compagnie Immobilière (1858) helped

95 James Rothschild (1792–1868), head of the Paris branch of the family

Baron Haussmann to rebuild the centre of Paris. Their Midi Railway (1852) linked Bordeaux, Toulouse and Cette and provided south-west France with a railway system joining Spanish lines at Bayonne and Perpignan. Their investments in France's new land-mortgage bank – the Crédit Foncier – helped to strengthen it. The skill with which they had once reconciled conflicting interests in the railway industry was again in evidence in their amalgamation of six rival gasworks and in the unification of the Paris omnibus services. They subscribed to government loans to help finance Louis Napoleon's wars in the Crimea, Italy and Mexico.

The Pereires also promoted many enterprises abroad – particularly railways in relatively underdeveloped countries such as Spain, Austria and Russia. In Spain they secured concessions to build what was to become the North of Spain Railway Company, and Isaac Pereire, as chairman of the Paris committee of the company, had a large measure of control over this important enterprise. In Russia the Pereires were involved in founding the Great Russia Railway Company, an international enterprise which had grandiose plans to build lines from St Petersburg to Moscow, and from Moscow to the Crimea and Nijni-Novgorod. Isaac Pereire was one of the directors, and French firms were awarded contracts to build bridges for the company and supply locomotives and rolling-stock. In Austria the Crédit Mobilier, in association with two Vienna banks, formed a syndicate to purchase the Austrian State Railway and various nationalized industrial properties. The Pereires also inspired the formation, in Holland, Spain and Italy, of local banks similar in character to the Crédit Mobilier.

There were various reasons for the brothers' surprising failure in 1867: their financial resources were overstretched; too much of the limited capital available to the Crédit Mobilier was invested in subsidiary companies, and when one of these firms – the Crédit Immobilier de Paris with a deficit of 113 million francs – failed, the public began to doubt the soundness of the Crédit Mobilier itself. The situation was aggravated by the hostility of the Rothschild Bank and by the folly of the Pereires in alienating the Bank of France by challenging its monopoly of the issue of banknotes. The Pereires were also at fault in issuing over-confident annual reports on the financial state of their bank, in paying some dividends out of capital instead of profits, and in indulging in reckless speculations in the shares of the Crédit Mobilier. In 1866, when its cash reserves were nearly exhausted, the bank doubled its capital from 60 to 120 million francs, but it was too late. Shortly before the opening of the Industrial Exhibition of 1867 there were persistent rumours in Paris concerning its dubious financial position. The bank's shares, which had once stood at 1,982 francs, fell to 140 francs, and the Pereire brothers were forced to resign. Although the Crédit Mobilier eventually failed, the ideas upon which it was based had a profound influence upon banking throughout the world.

FEUDAL ENTREPRENEUR ISTVÁN SZÉCHENYI

Feudal magnates and landed gentry who became entrepreneurs in the early industrial age, generally obtained their capital from the rents paid by their tenants, and from the raw materials, such as timber, iron, coal, wool and flax, available on their estates. The development of the linen, coal and iron industries of Silesia illustrates the working of this type of 'feudal capitalism'; the Lauchhammer ironworks in Saxony and the Waldstein woollen mills in Bohemia also owed their existence to aristocratic landowners. In Hungary, István Széchenyi was an entrepreneur of this kind.

Széchenyi's career shows how industrial progress could be made even in a relatively underdeveloped country like Hungary. As a young man serving in the army during the Napoleonic wars Széchenyi showed his business acumen as an agent of the family estates. He also speculated in salt, timber and hides. Between 1816 and 1825 he attempted to make good the deficiencies in his education by private reading and foreign travel. He studied Western institutions and, on his return, became the recognized leader of those who wished to create a new Hungary. For many years – indeed until Kossuth's rise to popularity – Széchenyi was a dominant figure in Magyar politics and a powerful advocate of constitutional reform.

Upon inheriting a share of his father's estates he turned his attention to their improvement. He imported thoroughbred stallions and mares from England and was largely responsible for founding a horse-racing society, which developed ten years later into the Hungarian National Agricultural Society. He imported cattle from Holland and pigs from Siberia. He produced better wool on his farms by improving his flocks of sheep, and was one of the first landowners in Hungary to plant mulberry trees so that silkworms could be raised. He used modern implements on his estate, drained swampy fields and modified the system of crop rotation by growing more potatoes and vegetables. The instructions which he gave to his steward Janos Lunkanyi in 1828 show that Széchenyi was determined to improve the lot of his serfs by allocating land for their personal use and by advising them on the most efficient methods of husbandry.

While engaged in improving his estates Széchenyi was also actively promoting public utilities and industrial undertakings. He became a member of the Diet in 1826 and six years later joined a committee which had been set up to found a commercial bank. He was the driving force behind the scheme and, after a long delay, had the satisfaction of seeing the establishment of the Hungarian Commercial Bank of Pest (1841). Strongly advocating the construction of a modern suspension bridge over the Danube, to link Buda and Pest, and replace the old bridge of boats, he persuaded a Viennese banker to support the project; and a bridge, designed by an English firm, was completed in 1849. Széchenyi was also appointed by the government to be the High Commissioner responsible for a scheme regulating navigation on the Danube at the Iron Gate. He was on the board of directors of the First Imperial Privileged

96, 97 The Hungarian statesman and feudal entrepreneur István Széchenyi (1791–1860); and a view of
the modern suspension bridge which he had built
across the Danube between Buda and Pest in 1849.
The regatta is in honour of the visiting
Emperor of Austria

Danube Shipping Company (1829) which ran a steamship
service between Vienna and Belgrade, and which controlled a
subsidiary company set up to run a shipyard at Altofen, a
suburb of Budapest. Another of his achievements was the
regulation of the River Tisza, by which 150 square miles of
lowlands was reclaimed. Széchenyi was also a member of a
group which sponsored the formation of a company to build a
railway on the right bank of the Danube from Budapest to
Vienna.

Széchenyi criticized those who regarded factories and steam
engines as 'infernal institutions'. He believed that Hungary
should follow the example of more advanced countries by
developing modern manufactures of her own. He himself
helped to promote the Pest Steam Flour Mill Company which
began operations in 1842. The steel-cylinder system of grinding

wheat – invented by the Swiss engineer Sulzberger – was used, and various experts were brought from Switzerland to operate the machines. A subsidiary firm, set up to service the machinery, had by 1847 become an independent engineering concern called Ganz and Company. As a landowner and entrepreneur – and also as a writer and a statesman – Széchenyi played a very important role in the economic and political development of Hungary between the end of the Napoleonic Wars and the Revolution of 1848.

RUSSIAN SERF–ENTREPRENEURS

At first sight the term 'serf-entrepreneur' appears to be a contradiction in terms. It might be supposed that in those parts of Europe where serfdom survived into the nineteenth century the role of the serfs in the early industrial age would be confined to that of factory workers. But the ability to start new manufacturing enterprises is not confined to any particular social group. In St Petersburg in the early nineteenth century there were a number of serfs who made annual cash payments (instead of rendering labour services) to the lord of the manor in their native villages. Some earned a living as porters, cab-drivers and shopkeepers, while others were skilled craftsmen – jewellers, locksmiths, shoemakers, candlemakers and tailors. Some of these men showed considerable entrepreneurial skill and in time built up flourishing businesses. In Russian villages the local craftsmen sometimes organized the sale of their products on a co-operative basis and those responsible for organizing an operation of this kind performed some of the functions of merchants and managers. For example, in 1850 there were five villages near Yaroslav where local craftsmen specialized in the manufacture of boxes, together producing some 150,000 a year.

Some Russian serfs succeeded in establishing industrial enterprises. At Ivanovo in the late eighteenth century a serf-entrepreneur named E. Grachev operated a linen manufactory and a calico-printing works on the estates of the Sheremetev family. He controlled over 500 looms for weaving flax, but four-fifths of his weavers worked in their own homes. His calico-printing works employed about 120 men. He installed spinning-jennies, calendering machines and roller-printing presses. By 1800 this firm had become one of the most important in Ivanovo. It owned four factories, constructed of stone, and seven dormitories, which served as living quarters for the operatives. Grachev, who had purchased his freedom for 130,000 roubles in 1795, became a wealthy man and invested in landed property in his own right.

In 1797 Savva Morosov, a serf on the estate of N. G. Ryumin, set up a small silk-ribbon workshop in the village of Zuevo (Bogorodski district) and shortly afterwards a second workshop. He supervised the looms while his wife was responsible for dyeing the silk cloth. In 1811 Morosov's enterprise was still a small one since it had only ten looms. For a while Napoleon's invasion of Russia and the burning of Moscow checked the expansion of the textile industries in this part of the country, but by 1820 Morosov was operating twice as many looms. At this time he extended his activities to the spinning and weaving of cotton, and farmed out the weaving to peasants living in near-by villages. In 1825 Morosov moved to Moscow, where he took advantage of the demand for cotton piece-goods, which had begun to increase at the same time that large quantities of Lancashire yarn – despite the high tariff of 1822 – became available at low prices. Morosov's factories produced both pure calico and cloth which was a mixture of cotton and wool. His two sons established factories of their own, which were, however, closely controlled by their father. In the early 1850s an inventory of the various Morosov enterprises showed that the family had 74 power-looms, 456 hand-looms and an annual output valued at nearly 2 million roubles. By the close of the nineteenth century the firm had developed into one of the largest in Moscow, employing 22,000 operatives and producing goods worth 32 million roubles.

IV THE WORKERS

98 Crest used by the Dewsbury,
Batley Heavy Woollen Weavers Association

The Industrial Revolution had dramatic consequences for all groups of the workers. The operatives in the factories, the miners in the collieries, the artisans in their workshops, and the peasants on the land had to adjust themselves to an entirely new way of life. Many entered the factories with great reluctance. To respectable craftsmen the factories appeared to be attracting workers of the lowest calibre and such establishments came to be regarded as little better than prisons or workhouses. The social evils of the mills, mines and manufacturing towns and the tragedies of jobless domestic workers who fell on evil days were among the first aspects of the new order to command the attention of reformers.

Many of the workers in the early factories were completely in the power of their new employers. In the eighteenth century many Scottish coal-miners and saltworkers were serfs. So were the workers in various mines and factories on the Continent, particularly those run by feudal magnates in Russia, Silesia and Bohemia. Even after the serfs had been emancipated there were workers who enjoyed little freedom. In the early nineteenth century a Durham miner or a Staffordshire potter who had signed a contract for a year and lived in a tied cottage was completely at the mercy of his master. There were other ways in which some employers were able to control their workers. In certain industrial districts it was not uncommon for men to draw wages before they had been earned and so fall permanently into debt. Workers in factories and mines were not only in their master's power but came under public control. They were forbidden to join trade unions, to go on strike or to emigrate. In France for much of the nineteenth century the workers had to carry identity cards, which enabled their employers and the police to check their movements and changes of employment.

Workers found it difficult to adapt themselves to the discipline imposed in the factories. Craftsmen and peasants had worked long hours in the past, but had been able to rest from time to time. The remorseless machine, however, needed constant attention. Punctuality and strict attention to work were enforced by fines and the threat of dismissal.

The new industrial system ruined the health of many workers. Almost every industry had its characteristic illnesses and physical deformities. Potters, painters and file-cutters suffered from lead-poisoning; miners from consumption, anaemia, eye strain and spinal deformities; grinders from asthma; spinners from bronchial disorders; and match-workers from phosphorus-poisoning. Jules Simon, writing about the French mills, declared that 'visitors cannot breathe in these sad places'. In continental countries which introduced conscription it was found that recruits from industrial regions had many more physical defects than young men from the country districts. The expectation of life of factory workers and miners was very short. It has been established that in the Sheffield cutlery industry in 1865 the average age of scissors-grinders was 32

99 Russian serfs on the Don. An early nineteenth-century attempt to convey the inhumanity of serfdom—an institution not abolished in Russia until 1861

years, of edge-tool and wool-shear grinders 33 years, of table-knife grinders 35 years, while out of 290 razor-grinders then working only 21 had reached 50 years of age.

Moreover, many accidents occurred in factories and mines. Falls of coal and underground explosions were frequent causes of death and injury in the mines. In the Ruhr, for example, fatal accidents rose from 26 in 1850 to 537 in 1900. And in the days when machinery was rarely fenced, it was inevitable that operatives should receive serious injuries. Builders, dockers, navvies and seamen were also engaged in dangerous occupations. Engels, writing about the English factory districts in 1844, declared that 'the health of whole generations of workers is undermined, and they are racked with disease and infirmities'.

100 Industrial accidents and occupational diseases plagued the lives of workers in the mines and factories of the nineteenth century. Employers generally took little interest in working conditions and few safety measures were enforced; the first compulsory state-insurance law was not passed until 1884. Left, a crowd gathering at the pit head of the Oaks colliery at Barnesly, 1866, is greeted by a second explosion

101 Polish miners descending a mine-shaft at Wielliczka display an appalling lack of safety consciousness: their worn rope, soft hats and naked candle flames are invitations to disaster

One of the most unfortunate social consequences of the early factory system was the exploitation of women and children. Before the Industrial Revolution they had been employed in domestic workshops. In Lyons in 1777 there were 3,823 children engaged in the manufacture of silks out of a total labour force of 9,657. In the age of machinery and steam-power, however, women and children were employed on an even larger scale than before, and the intensity of their work increased. But not all industries drew upon female labour. Few if any women worked in foundries or forges, for example. But in the textile trades the new inventions and processes frequently made it possible to reduce the number of men employed and to replace them by lower-paid women and children. When calico-printing was introduced into the English cotton industry there was a sudden increase in the number of boys employed. In one Lancashire mill in 1794 fifty-five apprentices worked side by side with only two journeymen. The wretched servitude imposed upon parish apprentices in the Lancashire cotton-mills was an early concern of humanitarian reformers in England.

102 The weariness of the cotton-yarn winder. The posture of a young girl in a Nottingham mill hints at the long hours and dreary lot of the nineteenth-century factory-worker

103 Women employed as heavy manual labourers for less than two shillings a day shovel gold-ore at the Troitzk mines, Siberia, 1906

At the end of the Napoleonic Wars inquiries concerning the labour force of forty-one Scottish and forty-eight Manchester mills showed that half the workers were children. In 1844 an examination of 412 Lancashire mills showed that 52 per cent of the workers were women. Millowners paid women and children less than men and found that they were generally more amenable to the discipline of the factory system.

Nassau Senior declared that a Parliamentary Report of 1842 on child labour in England disclosed 'the most frightful picture of avarice, selfishness and cruelty on the part of masters and parents, and of juvenile and infantile misery, degradation and destruction ever presented'. Shortly afterwards Dr Villermé's report on the French textile mills sharply criticized the exploitation of women and children. He wrote: 'Look at them as they come to town in the morning and leave in the evening. Among them are many women, pale and thin, walking barefoot through the mud. . . . And there are also young children – still more in number than the women – not less pale, not less

127

104 A view of Sheffield
from the south-east,
1858

dirty, covered in rags, greasy with the oil of the looms, which
has splashed on them while they worked.'

The most serious complaints of the workers in factories and
mines concerned long hours, low wages, fines and the truck
system, whereby employers paid in kind, not cash. Men,
women and children worked twelve hours or more a day and
were often totally exhausted when they went home. Since it
paid factory-owners to run machinery continuously, night-
shifts were introduced in certain industries. The number of
days worked in the year was increased. Sometimes Sunday
work was introduced, despite the protests of the Churches. In
districts where it had been customary for apprentices to have
Mondays free, employers did their best to abolish the practice.
And in Catholic countries the holidays on saints' days were
gradually reduced in the factories. Moreover, after the Industrial

Revolution a worker might have to travel a considerable distance on foot to get to work, whereas under the domestic system he had worked at home.

Wages, generally very low to begin with, were reduced in various ways: workers were fined for lateness or spoiled work; if wages were paid not in cash but in vouchers exchangeable at the employer's shop, the worker often found that he had to buy adulterated groceries and shoddy goods at inflated prices. Furthermore, if trade was slack the employers quickly reduced wages in order to cut their costs. The earnings of many workers – even of whole families – were often insufficient to pay the rent or to feed and clothe the family. It was not surprising that women and children went to work or that, even when they had jobs, factory operatives had to rely upon charity and poor relief to supplement their earnings. Since they could afford nothing better, the workers lived in damp, overcrowded, unhealthy cottages or flats – sometimes even in attics, cellars and outhouses. Their clothes were shabby and their food inadequate. The public house was their only refuge from the discomforts of their homes.

Conditions in the working-class districts of industrial towns were no better than conditions in the factories. The back-to-back houses and squalid courts in England and the equally sordid block of flats on the Continent soon deteriorated into slums. St Giles in London, Little Ireland in Manchester, the Voigtland in Berlin, the suburbs of Saint-Georges and Croix-Rousse in Lyons were all working-class quarters, in which the inhabitants enjoyed none of the amenities of civilized habitations. Lack of pure water and lavatories, inadequate sewerage and the absence of arrangements for the disposal of garbage made the industrial towns exceedingly insanitary places. The worst slums housed minority groups – the Irish in Liverpool and Manchester, the Poles in the Ruhr – who came from countries where the standard of living was actually lower than the deplorable standards of the industrial towns.

Some workers enjoyed better housing conditions than others. Engels, writing in 1844, described the incredible squalor in which the Manchester Irish lived by the River Medlock, and at the confluence of the Irk and the Irwell, but when he visited Ashton-under-Lyne, only a few miles away, he found that 'the streets are broader and cleaner, while the new bright-red cottages give every appearance of comfort'. Bad housing conditions know no national frontiers. Over half a century after Engels had described housing conditions in England, Lorenz Pieper, in a book on the Ruhr miners, devoted a chapter to the similar situation in the Ruhr district. He reported that in Hörde in 1896 an official inspection of 106 blocks of flats revealed that 19 were structurally unsound, 15 were unhealthy and 6 were quite unfit for human habitation. In Essen 17 per cent of the people lived in attics and a local building inspector found that 2,200 attics suffered from serious defects. On an

105 The home environment of the working classes: Gustave Doré's drawing of a London slum district straddled by rail viaducts (1870s)

estate near Wattenscheid it was reported in 1902 that a farmer had let a derelict outhouse to 17 families comprising 94 people.

Harsh discipline, excessive hours, low wages and poor accommodation did not exhaust the evils of the new industrial system. There was little security of employment. This was no new problem since vagabondage – sometimes on a large scale – had been common in rural societies in the past. With the coming of modern industry many workers found themselves in casual or seasonal employment: labourers on the land, at ports and harbours, and on construction works were often engaged by the day; builders were busier in the summer than in the winter; ironworks and textile mills which depended upon water-power

106 Nature, man and machine. *The Quarry* (1896) by Rousseau, in which an enigmatic denizen of the machine age dominates a French landscape

had to close if there was not enough water to drive the wheel which set the machinery in motion. Alfred Krupp's cry, 'If only I had sufficient water to work my hammer for a single day', was echoed by many other ironmasters in the early machine age. A severe winter might bring industrial production to a standstill if the roads were impassable. Sometimes, however, workers would be able to return to their villages when trade was slack in the industrial towns. Rural craftsmen sometimes divided their time between industry and agriculture. A survey of a rural French district (Sobre le Château) in 1848 mentioned that 'woolcombers like to work in the fields in the summer and return to the workshops in the autumn'.

Even workers who were engaged in branches of manufacture which were free from casual or seasonal work could not hope for regular employment, because the whole industrial economy was subject to fluctuations in trade. Masters and men became all too familiar with a trade cycle in which slumps occurred every ten years or so until the 1870s, when the brief crisis was replaced by a prolonged depression. For the worker a slump might mean a period of short time or unemployment extending over many months, during which he had to rely for his food and clothing upon public relief or private charity. At times of extreme crisis public works such as the National Workshops in Paris in 1848, might be undertaken to relieve unemployment.

107 A Victorian idealization of the manual labourer and his condition. A detail of *Work* (1863), by Ford Madox Brown

108 Victims of the cotton famine in Lancashire exchange tickets for food at a store run by a provident society (1861)

Since the Industrial Revolution took place in Britain earlier than elsewhere, it was here that the phenomenon of the trade cycle was first observed. But when other countries became industrialized they too suffered the same disagreeable experience. The growth of an international economy caused the evil effects of trade slumps in industrial countries to spread to agrarian and tropical regions which were engaged in the production of foodstuffs and raw materials. The great commercial crisis of 1857 was the first world slump.

Booms and slumps occurred so regularly that they could be predicted with some accuracy. It was natural that economists should take the view that each cycle followed precisely the pattern of the ones that had gone before. Although there was a rhythm of industrial activity – a phase of prosperity giving way to one of depression – each boom and slump had its own individual characteristics. In the early 1850s western Europe experienced a boom which owed much to a sudden influx of gold from California and Australia, while the crisis in the cotton industries ten years later was due to events on the other side of the Atlantic, namely the Civil War in the United States. Neither the gold discoveries nor the Civil War fit very neatly into any universal pattern of industrial booms and slumps. Karl Marx argued that a study of the trade cycle showed the existence of a permanent pool of unemployed labour which, in his view, was essential to the new industrial society.

The great Lancashire Cotton Famine illustrates the consequences of a trade depression. In 1860 there were about 2,000 cotton factories in the Lancashire-Cheshire manufacturing region. They had over 300,000 power-looms and over 20 million spindles and their labour force amounted to 500,000 operatives who earned £11 million a year. At this time Britain manufactured nearly half of the world's cotton yarn and piece-goods and the annual exports of the industry were valued at £46 million.

The cotton industry was one of the largest and most flourishing in the country but its prosperity was threatened by periodic slumps, owing to increased competition from abroad and undue dependence upon one source of supply – the cotton-plantations of the United States – for over three-quarters of its raw material. The outbreak of the Civil War in 1861 was followed by a blockade of the southern United States ports. The States of the Confederacy were cut off from the outside world and Lancashire could not secure its normal supplies of cotton. The result was that manufacturers eventually had to work short time or close their mills. It was estimated that the net loss of trade to the industry during the cotton famine amounted to over £60 million.

For the operatives the cotton famine was a period of short time, unemployment and distress. By November 1862 the Poor Law authorities were relieving over a quarter of a million people in the cotton districts. In 1863 the Public Works Act

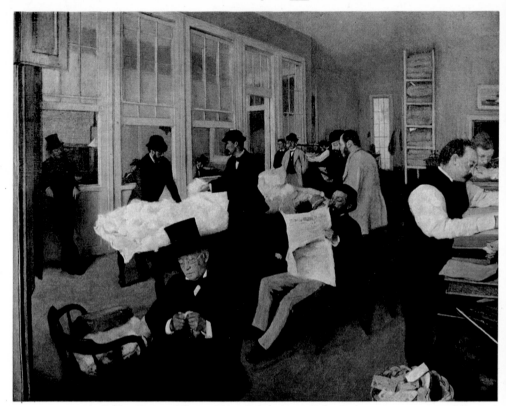

109 *The Cotton Office at New Orleans* (1873), by Degas. Cotton manufacturers in Europe depended on raw material from the United States

was passed to enable local authorities to borrow money on the
security of the rates to relieve unemployment by starting public
works. Ninety local authorities borrowed about £1 million
from the Public Works Loan Commissioners. But they gave
employment to only about 4,000 operatives which was a
mere fraction of the total number of unemployed factory
workers. Relief committees were set up in the distressed cotton
districts and their work was co-ordinated by a Central Relief
Committee in Manchester. Two national funds were established, one sponsored by the Lord Mayor of London. Altogether
over £1 million was raised for the relief of distress in Lancashire
at this time.

A few employers were well aware of the social problems following in the train of industrialization and sought to treat their workers in a humane and civilized way. Enlightened factory-owners reduced excessive hours, paid wages a little above the average, and provided their workers with canteens, reading-rooms, decent cottages and welfare services. Robert Owen, for example, turned the New Lanark cotton-mills into a model factory in the early years of the nineteenth century. He introduced a ten-hour working day, did not employ very young children, and provided various amenities for the operatives and their families.

In 1851 the woollen manufacturer Titus Salt began to build the model town of Saltaire near Bradford for his 3,000 operatives. He provided well-built houses, proper sanitation, a park, a hospital, schools, churches and public baths. At the same time some progressive employers at Mulhouse in Alsace assisted a society to build cottages which workers could buy over a period of years. This 'workers' city' had public wash-houses and baths, a communal kitchen and its own school – all paid for with the aid of a government grant. Within a few years similar 'workers' cities' had been built in France, Germany and Switzerland.

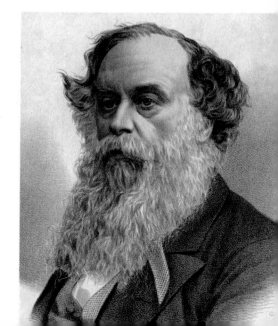

110, 111 Robert Owen and Titus Salt

But for one enlightened employer like Robert Owen or Titus Salt there were a hundred who ignored the plight of their workers. These employers had to be compelled by the State to improve conditions. The protests of the workers themselves and the sympathetic support of humanitarian reformers, such as Lord Shaftesbury, eventually brought about legislative reforms to ameliorate the worst social evils of the Industrial Revolution. In England attempts were made in 1802 and 1819 to limit the excessive hours worked by children in cotton-mills. The Truck Act of 1831 provided for the payment of all wages in cash. Althorp's Act of 1833, which applied to textile mills (excluding silk- and lace-works) forbade the employment of children under the age of nine, limited the hours of those aged between nine and eighteen, and prohibited night-work for children and young people. Inspectors were appointed to enforce the law. The compulsory registration of births after 1837 enabled inspectors to check the ages of factory children. The Collieries Act of 1842 prohibited the employment of women and children underground. In 1847 the Ten Hours Act limited the working week of women and young people to 58 hours of which no more than 10 might be worked in any one day. In effect, this also limited the hours worked by men. New factory laws of 1864 and 1867 covered many trades, such as the pottery trade, in which the workers had formerly enjoyed no protection.

In France a Law of 1841 fixed the minimum age at which children might be employed in factories at eight years, and limited the hours of work of factory children. In 1851 a law concerning apprentices gave some protection to certain young people who had not been included in the earlier enactment. But it was not until 1874 that more radical and more effective legislation was passed. The minimum age of factory children was raised to twelve and women workers also received some protection against exploitation by employers. In Prussia a decree of 1839 forbade the employment of children aged

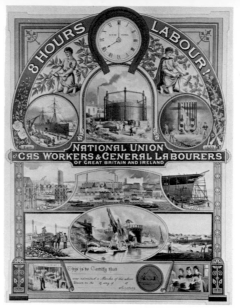

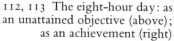

112, 113 The eight-hour day: as an unattained objective (above); as an achievement (right)

under nine in mines and factories, and limited the labour of young people under sixteen to ten hours. Moreover, young people were not allowed to work at night, on Sundays or on public holidays. In Russia it was not until 1882 that an edict was issued ending employment of children under the age of twelve and limiting the hours worked by young people (aged between twelve and fifteen) to eight.

To make early factory legislation effective was a slow process in all industrial countries. The laws were often limited to women, children and young people so that the adult worker still lacked legal protection. The first regulations were sometimes limited to a narrow range of industrial establishments, such as textile mills in England and factories employing over twenty people in France. The determined opposition of the more reactionary employers often delayed the full implementation of the law, and factory inspectors fought an uphill battle to enforce new regulations.

Working-class conditions were improved in other ways besides factory legislation. When it was realized that the rich could die from cholera or typhus as easily as the poor, measures were taken to clean up the industrial towns. The cholera

139

epidemic of 1831–2 affected places as far apart as Riga, Hamburg, Sunderland, London and Paris. The next epidemics were in 1848–9 and in 1854 when over 70,000 people died in England and Wales alone. Although the English Public Health Board of 1848 was ineffective, the municipal authorities gradually improved the urban environment of the factory workers. Liverpool was the first English city to appoint a Medical Officer of Health (1847). Birmingham's housing and sanitation were greatly improved when Joseph Chamberlain was Mayor between 1873 and 1875. In London it was the Metropolitan Board of Works (1855) and the water undertakings, amalgamated to form the Metropolitan Water Board (1902), which improved the amenities. A good supply of water was provided; countless cesspools were removed; slums were pulled down; and open-air spaces were preserved.

The condition of factory workers was also improved by advances in medical knowledge, by the expansion of hospital services, by the preservation of commons, and by the establishment of municipal wash-houses and baths. Drunkenness declined when intoxicating liquor was heavily taxed and when hours of drinking in public houses were restricted. Police forces were established and penal systems reformed. Towns were lit at night, first by gas and then by electricity. When elementary education became compulsory, children could no longer be employed in factories, and their opportunities for advancement increased.

Towards the end of the nineteenth century the first workers' insurance schemes were inaugurated. Until then the breadwinner who suffered an injury, fell ill or could not find work received no subsistence allowance. In 1883 Germany under Bismarck led the way by providing compulsory insurance against sickness, accidents and old age for factory workers, miners and the lower-paid black-coated workers. Operating through existing and newly established friendly societies, the scheme was financed by weekly contributions from employers and workers, and its benefits included free medical attention

140

114 Membership certificate of the Associated Shipwrights' Society showing welfare benefits to which members were entitled ▶

and a'weekly payment during illness. In 1884 the Accident Insurance Law was passed. Financed entirely by the employers, who now had a strong incentive to make their factories as safe as possible, it provided that a worker injured in the factory or mine would receive medical and financial benefits similar to those included in the health scheme, and that the widow of the victim of a fatal industrial accident would receive a burial grant, a pension, and an allowance for dependent children. An old-age and disability pension scheme was founded in 1889 and financed by equal contributions from employers and workers, with the State contributing 50 Marks a year for each insured person. Under this scheme a small old-age pension became payable to a worker upon his reaching the age of seventy.

Similar schemes were later adopted by other countries. In Britain the Workmen's Compensation Act (1906), the Old Age Pensions Act (1908) and the National Insurance Act (1911) gave workers the same sort of protection as that enjoyed by the Germans under Bismarck's schemes. The British Unemployment Insurance Act (1911), however, took matters a step further by providing grants to the unemployed – at first only to men in the building and engineering trades, but later to other workers as well.

THE SELF-HELP MOVEMENT

The State was by no means entrusted with the whole task of dealing with the social problems accompanying industrialization; to improve their conditions the workers frequently took the initiative themselves. They did this by self-help, by forming trade unions, by political action, and even by violence. Although their hours were long and their wages low, there were those who studied to make up for lack of schooling, who provided for the future by putting money into savings banks and friendly societies, and who tried to raise their standard of living by taking advantage of various types of co-operative organizations.

The development of mechanics institutes in Britain may serve as an example of the way in which working men sought self-improvement through education. In 1799 George Birkbeck, of Anderson's University (Glasgow), was struck by the zeal for knowledge among the mechanics who made his scientific apparatus. 'Why are these minds left without the means of obtaining that knowledge which they so ardently desire,' he asked himself, 'and why are the avenues to science barred against them, because they are poor?' Birkbeck inaugurated free courses in science and mechanics, and when he left Scotland in 1804 they were continued by Andrew Ure, who later claimed that his students were 'spread over the kingdom as proprietors and managers of factories'.

In 1823 some students left Anderson's University to form their own mechanics institute, and shortly afterwards a similar institution was established in London. Lord Brougham and Francis Place were closely associated with the founding of the London Mechanics Institute and Birkbeck was its first President. Other institutes – some with excellent libraries and reading rooms – were set up in the provinces to provide artisans with the opportunity to study. In time, however, many mechanics institutes changed their character. Samuel Smiles observed in 1849 that the artisans had often been replaced by 'the middle and respectable classes'; and courses in scientific and technical subjects gave way to less demanding popular talks on literature and travel. In 1844 Engels had commented upon

the popularity of lectures on economics and on scientific and aesthetic topics which are frequently held at working-class institutes, particularly those run by socialists. I have sometimes come across workers, with their fustian jackets falling apart, who are better informed on geology, astronomy and other matters than many an educated member of the middle classes in Germany. No better evidence of the extent to which the British workers have succeeded in educating themselves can be brought forward than the fact that the most important modern works in philosophy, poetry and politics are in practice read only by the proletariat.

115 *New Discoveries in Pneumaticks!* (1802), a Gillray satire on the fashion of attending scientific lectures. Public lectures on educational topics were to become increasingly popular as the century wore on

Savings banks were established in the industrial countries to encourage thrift among the workers and to protect them from having to seek charity or public relief when they were sick or unemployed. Among the earliest of these banks were those set up by Priscilla Wakefield at Tottenham (1798) and Henry Duncan in Scotland, shortly afterwards. Soon a number of these 'frugality banks' – as Jeremy Bentham called them – had been established. They were not managed by the depositors, but by aristocratic or middle-class committees. Consequently they were viewed with some suspicion by the workers – Cobbett, for example, was one of their critics – and the early depositors were self-employed artisans, shopkeepers and domestic servants rather than factory operatives. But eventually these banks did attract the savings of the workers. By 1828 more

144

than £14 million had been invested in savings banks; by 1850 the number of depositors had risen to over a million, and in 1861, a State savings bank, run by the Post Office, was established.

Britain's example was followed by France in 1818 when the Royal Maritime Insurance Company established a savings bank in Paris, the necessary capital being subscribed by private investors, a group of bankers and the Bank of France. In the next twelve years seventeen savings banks were founded in the main provincial cities. An analysis of the new depositors in the Paris savings bank in 1850 showed that most of them were workers. In Prussia the first savings bank was set up in Berlin and the deposits were guaranteed by the municipality. By 1847 the total deposits in the Prussian savings banks amounted to the equivalent of £2.25 million.

While savings banks were generally founded by philanthropists, employers, municipalities or the State, friendly societies were established and run by the workers themselves. The nineteenth-century friendly societies in Britain generally grew out of social clubs whose members paid a weekly subscription of a few pence and received sick benefits in return. At times when workers' organizations were banned, the friendly societies might serve as a cloak for underground trade-union activities.

By 1803 there were 9,600 societies in Britain with a total membership of over 700,000. In the course of the nineteenth century large friendly societies, consisting of many local branches, developed in the industrial districts, particularly in Lancashire. The Oddfellows had their headquarters in Manchester, the Rechabites in Salford, and the Ancient Shepherds in Ashton. By 1850 the Oddfellows had 400,000 members, many of them factory operatives. In France, too, there were many friendly societies supported by both craftsmen and factory workers and by 1845 the country had 1,900 such societies. The German friendly societies developed rather later and more slowly. Excluding the old-established miners' guilds, it appears that only fifty-four friendly societies were founded in Germany between 1801 and 1840. As industries expanded in Germany it was not unusual for factory-owners to establish friendly societies for their employees, but the workers had little if any control over their management. By 1880 about 2.6 million factory workers, miners and craftsmen were members.

THE CO-OPERATIVE SOCIETIES

The co-operative movement provides a further illustration of self-help among industrial workers, craftsmen and peasants. The four main types of enterprise fostered by the movement were retail shops, banks, industrial (producers') workshops, and farming co-operatives. C. R. Fay has observed that 'Great Britain took the lead in the store movement because she was the first to possess, as the result of the Industrial Revolution, a distinctive working class, which proceeded to organize itself as wage-earners in a trade union and as wage-spenders in a co-operative store.' Retail co-operative stores were set up after the Napoleonic Wars and by 1833 about 400 societies were in existence. By that time the movement was sufficiently developed to hold annual congresses and support a journal called the *Co-operator*. The credit for establishing retail stores is generally given to some twenty-eight Rochdale weavers who opened their tiny shop in Toad Lane in December 1844 and registered it as a friendly society. But similar co-operative societies had been in existence for some time. The main claim to fame of the 'Rochdale Pioneers' was that they successfully operated the 'dividend' system. Trading surpluses were returned to the members of the society in proportion to their purchases, and so the customers obtained the profits which might otherwise have been pocketed by the owners of private shops.

The co-operative movement spread throughout the industrial regions of England and Scotland, its popularity attributable to the payment of the 'dividend', to the democratic method of administration (one vote for each member however many

116 A meeting of the Manchester and Salford Co-operative Society, 1865 ▶

shares he held), and to the firm stand taken against the sale of shoddy or adulterated goods. The financial stability of the British co-operative societies was strengthened by the introduction of a system whereby a member could withdraw his dividend only if he held at least five £1 shares in the society. The dividend was used to buy shares by instalments until £5 had been invested. In 1851 there were about 130 co-operative stores in Britain mainly in the north of England and in Scotland, many of them still quite small enterprises. An Act of 1862, however, allowed co-operative societies to register as limited liability companies, and as they could now invest money in one another it was possible for them to join together to establish wholesale and producers' societies on a co-operative basis in England (Manchester, 1863) and Scotland (Glasgow, 1868).

The wholesale societies established factories, farms and planta-
tions to produce the foodstuffs and manufactured goods sold
in the retail stores. By 1881 there were 964 co-operative retail
stores in Britain with a total membership of 546,000. Although
it was essentially a working-class movement the British
co-operative societies received encouragement and help from
middle-class supporters, such as Robert Owen, J. F. D. Maurice
(the Christian-Socialist), G. J. Holyoake and E. Vansittart
Neale (the Secretary of the Co-operative Union of 1873).
The British co-operative movement strongly influenced similar
developments abroad. The policies of the important Schwanden
society in Switzerland (1863) and the Nîmes society in France
(1885) closely followed the British model.

Retail co-operative stores (*Konsum*) developed in a rather
different way in Germany. The first co-operative societies for
retail trade were established in the 1860s not, as in Britain, by
the workers themselves, but by philanthropic middle-class
reformers. To some extent they were regarded as poor relations
of the more active co-operative urban banks founded by
F. H. Schulze-Delitzsch; indeed some of the early German
co-operative retail stores were closely associated with co-
operative banks. By 1873 there were 189 co-operative societies
(affiliated to the German Co-operative Union) with a membership of 87,500. There may have been as many co-operators as
this in societies which were not affiliated to the Co-operative
Union. The period 1874–85, which was one of economic
depression, saw little progress in the co-operative movement.
After 1886, however, the fortunes of the co-operative retail
stores improved. A Law of 1889 enabled the societies to be
registered as limited liability companies and by 1900 the
membership of the affiliated societies had risen to half a million.
In 1894 the German Wholesale Co-operative Society was
established in Hamburg.

While retail co-operative stores started in Britain, co-operative banks originated in Germany in the 1850s. Schulze-
Delitzsch was the first to establish such banks in the towns while

F. W. Raiffeisen was the founder of land banks in the rural districts. While he was a Justice of the Peace and Mayor of the little town of Delitzsch in the Prussian province of Saxony, Schulze-Delitzsch was faced with the problem of distress among craftsmen, artisans and tradesmen. He saw that many of these workers did not earn enough to provide themselves and their families with adequate housing, food and clothing. In an effort to earn more money they were forced to work such long hours that their health suffered. Schulze-Delitzsch believed that thrift, organized on a co-operative basis, could eventually raise the workers' standard of living. In 1849 he established both a friendly society to provide sickness benefits and a co-operative association of shoemakers to buy leather. In the following year he set up his first co-operative 'bank' – a loan society of ten artisans. He considered that credit, provided by the accumulated savings of small investors, would enable craftsmen to improve their efficiency and increase their business.

By 1859 there were eighty co-operative urban banks in Germany and by the end of the nineteenth century every German city had its local co-operative bank. The capital of these banks consisted of members' shares, and deposits of various kinds from members and non-members. Credit, which was available only to members, could be obtained in the form of a loan or a discount of commercial bills of exchange. Borrowers had to provide security by a guarantee from a relation or friend, by a mortgage or by the deposit of collateral. The cardinal features of the Schulze-Delitzsch system were the personal pledge of security for a loan, the ownership of the bank by small shareholders, and the limiting of the bank's activities to a single town. An analysis of the membership of these banks in 1890 showed that 29·3 per cent of the members were farmers, 27·9 per cent craftsmen, 8·7 per cent shopkeepers, 11·6 per cent wage-earners, and 13·9 per cent professional men or pensioners.

The German co-operative banks which followed the model recommended by Raiffeisen were established in rural districts, and catered to the needs of smallholders, rural craftsmen and village shopkeepers. Raiffeisen, the Burgomaster of Neuwied, near Coblenz, established a co-operative society in 1848 to enable members to purchase potatoes and bread. He next set up a co-operative credit bank at Flammersfeld in the Westerwald. Most of the capital was provided by wealthy philanthropic farmers. Later Raiffeisen founded co-operative banks which were run by the members, generally smallholders.

There were differences between the organization of the Raiffeisen and Schulze-Delitzsch banks. Schulze-Delitzsch insisted that members of his banks should subscribe an adequate share capital. But Raiffeisen did not consider share capital to be of great importance; members of his banks were usually smallholders and their property – farmhouse, land and stock – provided all the security needed. The Raiffeisen banks were smaller than those of Schulze-Delitzsch. Raiffeisen believed that each co-operative bank should serve a single parish, and because the bank was so small it could generally be run from a private house by voluntary workers. Office buildings and salaried officials – which the Schulze-Delitzsch banks required – were rarely necessary. And since prospective borrowers were normally known personally to the members of the society, bad debts were very rare. Most of the loans made by the Raiffeisen banks were mortgages on the security of the land owned by the borrowers.

In 1876 a central credit bank for farming was set up to facilitate loans between agricultural co-operative societies. By 1890 Germany had 1,729 rural co-operative land banks. Many of them were in south-west Germany – the heart of a region dominated by small freeholders.

Two kinds of producers' co-operatives were established in western Europe in the nineteenth century: agricultural and industrial. The development of agricultural societies in Denmark may serve to show how the principle of co-operative buying and selling could be successfully applied to farming. The period of reconstruction in Denmark after the loss of Schleswig-

Holstein in 1864 saw a revival of national life that found expression in many forms, and co-operative societies were born during this period of reconstruction. Co-operation was ideally suited to the Danes, who were a people of dairy and pig farmers and smallholders dependent upon exports for their living. The first co-operative retail shop was founded in 1866 and this was followed by the establishment of producers' co-operatives – dairies, bacon-curing factories and egg-collecting centres. In 1906 the Danish dairy farmers were organized in over a thousand co-operative societies (157,000 members) which controlled the sale of four-fifths of the country's butter. Exports of butter were handled by nine co-operative agencies, and some of Copenhagen's milk was supplied by a co-operative society. Two-thirds of Denmark's bacon output was cured in thirty-three co-operative curing plants. The collection and marketing of eggs was handled partly by 500 societies specializing in this work and partly by bacon and butter societies.

In Germany a number of agricultural co-operatives were founded on the model of a society established by Haas in East Prussia in 1871. Originally membership had been confined to the owners of large estates and substantial farmers, but in 1885 some agricultural co-operatives of smallholders began to buy their feeding-stuffs and fertilizers through the Insterburg society. The Haas societies eventually established a national federation to deal on more equal terms with the cartels that controlled the supply of chemical fertilizers. Various specialized agricultural co-operatives were set up, such as those which purchased farm machinery or sold dairy produce, wine and cereals. In France farm syndicates developed in the 1880s. Their activities were a good deal wider in scope than agricultural co-operatives elsewhere, but they often assumed responsibility for the purchase of smallholders' requirements, and for the sale of their produce.

Industrial co-operative societies were confined to Britain, France and Italy and, on the whole, they were less successful than agricultural societies.

In France in the 1840s the socialist Louis Blanc advocated the establishment of producers' co-operative workshops. He argued that craftsmen could free themselves from the thraldom of capitalism by going into partnership to set up their own workshops. After the revolution of 1848, at the time of the Second Republic, some co-operative workshops were founded with the aid of a government grant of 3 million francs but few of them were successful. Only the society formed by a small group of spectacle-makers in Paris survived to the end of the nineteenth century. Under the Third Republic a fresh attempt was made to establish producers' co-operative workshops. In 1906, 338 such societies were in existence, one-third of them in or near Paris and Lyons. The largest group (112 societies) was engaged in various branches of the building trade. The State assisted the producers' co-operatives by subsidies (93,000 francs in 1905) and by granting them preferential treatment in tendering for government contracts. The building co-operative societies, for example, were awarded valuable contracts in connection with the Paris Exhibition of 1900.

There were similarities between the producers' co-operatives in France and the old-established *artels* in Russia. In the Russian villages it was not uncommon for peasant-artisans to co-operate in the buying of raw materials and the sale of finished articles. Sometimes they went into partnership to establish workshops, forges and foundries. In the construction industry various tradesmen, such as carpenters, joiners, masons and tilers, would form co-operative *artels* to erect a building. In Russian towns the porters, cab-drivers and newspaper-sellers were often organized in *artels*.

None of the associations of factory workers, craftsmen or peasants – educational institutes, savings banks, friendly societies, co-operatives – threatened the stability of the new society that emerged as a result of the Industrial Revolution. The workers' banks did not hamper the activities of the joint-stock banks; the co-operative retail shops did not stop the expansion of the multiple stores; and nothing came of the dreams of Louis

Blanc and Ferdinand Lassalle that co-operative workshops might one day threaten the fortunes of capitalist industrial enterprises.

Trade unions were workers' associations of a different kind from friendly or co-operative societies. In the days when goods were manufactured in small workshops a personal relationship existed between master and craftsman which could not survive the coming of large factories. When he took over his father's foundry, Alfred Krupp employed seven men, but at the end of his career his labour force numbered tens of thousands. A factory hand or miner was in no position to argue with his employer about wages or hours of work. The workers' bargaining power was strengthened if all the men in a factory or district combined to present a united front to their masters. Associations of workers had existed under the domestic system, but assumed greater significance when operatives were gathered together in large factories, since it was easier for men working together to form a union than for men scattered in a number of villages to do so. By threatening to strike, a trade union might secure better wages and improved working conditions, which no individual worker could hope to achieve by himself.

The employers, strongly opposed to trade unions, were sufficiently influential to have them outlawed. In Britain trade unions were prohibited by Acts of 1799 and 1800, in France by the Law of Le Chapelier (1791) and articles in Napoleon's Penal and Civil Codes, and in Russia by the Penal Code of 1845. When later, such enactments were modified or repealed, trade-union activities could still fall foul of the law. In England they could be prosecuted under the laws relating to masters and servants or, under the common law, for conspiracy. Six Dorset farm workers who joined a union were prosecuted under a Statute passed at the time of the Naval Mutiny of 1797. These men – the 'Tolpuddle martyrs' – were found guilty of administering illegal oaths and sentenced to transporation for seven years.

117 *The General Meeting* (c. 1830), an anti-trade-union cartoon questioning the competence of working-class assemblies to organize their own affairs

Associations of craftsmen had flourished in England in the eighteenth century. They fought for the maintenance of traditional piece-work rates and the continuation of customary restrictions upon the number of apprentices to be admitted to their trade. Sometimes they organized the provision of food and lodging for members who were tramping from one town to another in search of work, and they also helped members in times of unemployment or sickness. Even during the period of repressive legislation of 1799–1824 such unions had little to fear from the law. But attempts to form trade unions among the new factory operatives, such as the cotton-spinners, alarmed both the employers and the government. The efforts of Francis Place and Joseph Hume secured the repeal of the Anti-Combination Laws in 1824. This was followed by a wave of industrial unrest and a new Act was passed in 1825 which, while allowing trade unions to exist, forbade the intimidation of blacklegs and made it very difficult for unions to keep within the law when organizing a strike. Attempts were now made to establish trade unions among factory workers and miners on

154

118 *Gathering of the Unions on New-Hall Hill*, Birmingham, 1832 ▶

something more than a purely local basis. John Doherty established the National Union of Cotton-Spinners (1829) and the National Association for the Protection of Labour (1830). The latter claimed a membership of 100,000 among the textile workers of the north and east Midlands, but both unions collapsed after a few years.

While the cotton operatives of Lancashire were being organized by Doherty the coal-miners of Durham and Northumberland formed a union which called a strike in April 1831 when the coalowners proposed to reduce wages on the renewal of the miners' annual contracts. After seven weeks the owners gave way and granted wage increases and a reduction in the number of hours to be worked. But when the miners followed up this success with a second strike a year later the owners were ready for them and replaced the strikers by men from other mining areas. The miners resorted to violence and about fifty of them were punished at the local assizes. By September the strikers had to admit defeat and their union collapsed.

119 The Achilles heel of the early trade-unions was their lack of national co-ordination, and British employers challenged with strike action about

The failure of the cotton-spinners and the coal-miners was followed by the failure of Robert Owen's Grand National Consolidated Trades Union of 1833–4, which aimed at the organization of a general strike by all wage-earners so as to gain control of the economic system. The movement quickly collapsed, partly because of internal disputes, and partly because employers met the challenge to their authority by prosecuting a number of trade unionists.

For a time the English workers gave up their attempt to improve their conditions by industrial action, and turned instead to political action. They hoped that the passing of the Reform Bill of 1832 would lead to the election of a Commons

1830 were quick to exploit this weakness. As a result many workers in their frustration resorted to violence. Above, *Bristol During the Riots of 1831*

which would be prepared to listen to their grievances. They supported the movements in favour of a 'People's Charter', a ten-hour day, and the modification of the new Poor Law. When the Commons rejected the Charter for the second time in 1842 it became clear that little was being achieved by appealing to Parliament and there was a revival of trade-union activity, among both the cotton-spinners of Lancashire and the miners of Durham and Northumberland. In 1842 the labour unrest in Lancashire flared up in the Plug Plot riots. The coal-miners set up a new union at Wakefield in 1841 and, when they held their first National Convention at Manchester in January 1844, claimed a membership of over 60,000. The miners of

Durham and Northumberland – the largest and most militant group in the union – engaged the able solicitor W. P. Roberts as their legal adviser. In April 1844, when their annual contracts ran out, the northern miners refused to renew them on the old terms. Roberts drew up a proposed new contract to provide for a ten-hour day, a guarantee of work for four days in each week, the abolition of fines, and the introduction of a contract for six instead of twelve months. The owners, however, broke the strike by importing blacklegs into the Newcastle coalfield and by turning the men out of their tied cottages. After nineteen weeks the men went back to work virtually on the owners' terms. But they had achieved one success. The annual contract disappeared and the miners were now hired on a monthly contract.

The failure of the Plug Plot riots in Lancashire and the miners' strike in Durham and Northumberland – followed by the final collapse of Chartism in 1848 – marked the closing of the early phase in the history of English trade-unionism. In the middle of the nineteenth century the centre of gravity of the trade-union movement shifted from the north to London and its leadership in the future lay with highly skilled and relatively well-paid workers, such as engineers. The Amalgamated Society of Engineers (1851) was typical of the 'new model' unionism of 1850–70. These unions, led by men like William Newton, William Allan, Daniel Guile, Edward Coulson and George Odger, were organized on a national basis, levied fairly high subscriptions, appointed full-time officials, provided unemployment and health benefits and tried to settle industrial disputes by negotiation rather than by strikes. Their secretaries, whose headquarters were in London, worked closely together, and this 'junta' exercised a considerable influence in moulding the policy of the trade-union movement. It played a part in founding the Trades Union Congress in 1868. At about the same time machinery to settle industrial disputes by conciliation or arbitration was successfully established by A. J. Mundella in the Nottingham hosiery industry and Judge R. A. Kettle in the Wolverhampton building trade. The significance of the new 'amalgamated societies' and the 'junta' should not, however, be exaggerated. They represented a minority within the trade-union movement, and in many industries control of the unions rested wholly with the local organizations, which were frequently very vigorous in their pursuit of the workers' interests. Trade-union militancy in the 1850s led to the strikes of the engineers (1852), the Preston cotton operatives (1853) and the London building workers (1859–60).

In 1865–6 the public was reminded of the survival of the darker side of the trade-union movement. People were shocked to read in the newspapers of the outrages perpetrated against non-unionists and employers by certain workers in the Sheffield cutlery industry.

A Parliamentary Inquiry of 1867 proved the complicity of the Saw Grinders Union – and its Secretary, William Broad-head – in instigating and paying for various outrages, which included the blowing up of Wheatman and Smith's saw factory, the murder of James Linley (who had displeased the union by taking on too many apprentices), and many brutal assaults upon non-unionists who had acted as strike-breakers.

One result of the inquiry into the Sheffield outrages was the enactment of a law in 1871 which made practically all forms of picketing illegal. Trade unionists strongly criticized a measure which they regarded as a reactionary attempt to make strikes impossible and their opposition contributed to the modification of the law in 1875. Peaceful – as distinct from violent – picketing was now allowed. Another Act of 1871 was more favourable to the future development of the unions since it protected their funds from embezzlement. In the early 1870s the membership of trade unions in Britain probably amounted to about one-tenth of the male working population, but the period from 1871 to 1914 saw a great expansion of trade unionism. Although Joseph Arch's agricultural labourers' union of 1872 was crushed by the landlords and farmers,

120 London match workers marching to Westminster to present an unsuccessful petition for a minimum wage and better working conditions, 1871

Ben Tillett's union of London dockers secured a minimum wage of 6*d* an hour as a result of a strike in 1889, while Annie Besant's efforts to organize the London match girls had also achieved a measure of success in 1888. The new unions of the 1880s were generally associations of poorly paid unskilled or semi-skilled workers. Their members could afford only low subscriptions and enjoyed few friendly-society benefits. These unions were more militant than those established in the 1850s. Moreover, their leaders believed in political as well as industrial action, and they were closely associated with the organizations that eventually developed into the Labour Party. When Labour Members were elected to Parliament they often received financial support from the unions. By 1900 the total membership of British trade unions had risen to over two million.

Early in the twentieth century enemies of the organized workers attacked trade unions through the courts. The Taff Vale Railway Company was awarded £23,000 damages in 1901 against the Amalgamated Society of Railway Servants for revenue lost during a strike – although the strike had not been authorized by the union. In 1906, however, the Trades Disputes Act protected unions from similar actions. In 1909 W. V. Osborne won an action against a trade union (of which he was an official), restraining it from collecting a political levy to support Labour Members of Parliament. Had this judgement been allowed to stand, the activities of the Labour Party would have been seriously restricted. An Act of 1909 provided for the payment of Members of Parliament, while an Act of 1913 legalized the political levy, provided that no trade unionist was forced to contribute.

121 Some of the workers at the factory of Bryant and May involved in the successful 'Matchgirls' strike' of 1888 organized by Annie Besant

161

Elsewhere in Europe the growth of trade unions was hampered by legal restrictions. Some old-established workers' organizations – the miners' guilds in Germany, the journeymen's guilds in France and the *artels* in Russia – were allowed to survive into the new industrial age, but the more modern unions of craftsmen and factory workers were often driven underground by the hostility of employers and governments. In France many early workers' associations disguised themselves as friendly societies. In Lyons in the 1830s a similar type of union was evolved – the *devoir mutuel* – and this played an important part in the organization of two workers' risings in the city. During Louis-Philippe's reign there were over a thousand strikes followed by prosecutions before the courts.

122 French reverses during the Franco–Prussian War of 1870–1 precipitated the fall of Napoleon III. Left, Prussian guns bombard Paris during the siege which brought the war to an end

It was not until 1868 that the government of Napoleon III gave the French workers partial recognition of the right to combine to protect their interests. It was a time of industrial unrest. In the previous year there had been a bitter strike in the Roubaix cotton industry, accompanied by violence. The workers resisted both wage reductions and an attempt by the factory-owners to make weavers operate two looms instead of one. The government thereupon announced that in future the authorities would no longer enforce the prohibition of trade unions, although no change in the law was proposed. This concession was followed by a number of strikes. One of the most serious was at the Le Creusot steelworks early in 1870, when 3,000 troops were sent to maintain order. The trade-

163

123 Left, *The Barricade*, a lithograph by Steinlen evoking the horror and violence which attended the liquidation of the Paris Commune of 1871—by a French army, with Prussia's consent

124 The summary execution of a Communard, depicted in a lithograph by Manet also entitled *The Barricade* ▶

union movement in France suffered a new setback when France was defeated by Germany in 1870–1 and the Second Empire collapsed. The Paris workers rose in revolt against the new régime and set up a rival administration of their own – the Commune. The bloody liquidation of the Commune was followed by a wave of repression of socialists and trade unionists, and once more the workers' organizations – whether industrial or political in character – were driven underground.

The French syndicates had to wait until 1884 before they received legal recognition and were allowed to engage in trade-union activities. But they did not make the same progress as the English and German trade unions. Only a relatively small proportion of the workers who were eligible to join actually did so. One reason for the weakness of the workers' movement was the fact that the French socialists were split into warring factions, and their dissensions were reflected in rivalries among trade unionists. Another reason was the reluctance of the workers to subscribe enough 'resistance money' to their unions.

An English worker remarked that at meetings of the First International the French delegates were the first to raise their hands to vote for a resolution but the last to put their hands into their pockets when a subscription was due. Charles Rist calculated that in 1911 the average annual trade-union subscription in France was a mere 2.76 francs, compared with 42.50 francs in England and 32.60 francs in Germany. In the circumstances it was not surprising that in the early years of the twentieth century the French trade-union movement should have fallen under the domination of a group of militant 'syndicalists', who preached and practised the doctrine of violence, strikes and revolution, rather than progress by peaceful negotiations with their employers. The grave social unrest in France on the eve of the First World War was due, not only to the grievances of many workers, but also to the failure of the French workers to establish a really stable and powerful trade-union organization.

In Germany it was not until the 1860s that both the political and industrial sides of the workers' movement showed signs of revival. Trade unions of craftsmen and factory workers were established – sometimes disguised as friendly societies or social clubs. In Saxony, where the workers secured the right to form trade unions in 1861, the printers of Leipzig went on strike in 1865 and secured an increase in wages for apprentices. A wave of strikes followed in the building trades of Berlin and Hamburg. The north German industrial code of 1869 legalized workers' combinations but safeguarded the rights of those who did not wish to join a union or to take part in a strike. The most important associations were the 'free' unions which generally adopted model statutes, drawn up by August Bebel, and were closely associated with the Social Democrat Party. Of less significance were the Hirsch-Duncker or 'radical' unions – the first was established in 1868 – which were less militant and tried to settle industrial disputes by conciliation rather than by strikes. Originally they were loosely linked with the Progressive Party but when this party declined as a political force its influence over the 'radical' unions also declined. At about the same time Wilhelm Ketteler, the Bishop of Mainz, was advocating the organization of Catholic workers, and eventually 'Christian' unions were set up – largely under the aegis of the Catholic Church – in the hope of preventing workers from being infected by socialist doctrines. Finally, there were 'yellow' or 'peaceful' associations which were not trade unions in the normal sense since they were company unions, founded and subsidized by the employers.

The 'free' socialist unions had to fight hard for survival but their tenacity and sacrifices were eventually rewarded and they secured the support of the majority of the German workers. In the 1870s they struggled for their existence against the attacks of powerful industrialists, such as Emil Kirdorf and Alfred Krupp in the Ruhr and Stumm in the Saar, and were faced with the implacable hostility of Bismarck. The Anti-Socialist Law of 1878 hit the 'free' unions as hard as the Social Democrat Party. About a hundred were dissolved, while others had to turn themselves into non-political bodies or friendly societies. To make matters worse Puttkamer, the reactionary Prussian Minister of the Interior, used the Anti-Socialist Law to outlaw strikes in 1886. Three years later there was a wave of strikes in the mining districts of the Ruhr, the Saar and Upper Silesia. There were serious disorders in the Ruhr and troops were called in. In the resulting clashes between strikers and soldiers eleven people were killed and twenty-six injured.

The 'free' trade unions, like the Social Democrat Party, survived all attempts to suppress them. In 1891 there were 343,200 trade unionists in Germany, of whom 277,000 belonged to the 'free' unions. In the 1890s German workers recovered their right to form trade unions though this did not apply to farm labourers, seamen or domestic servants. The 'free' unions, like the British unions, levied fairly high subscriptions and established a National Congress to strengthen their position when dealing with employers or the government. On the eve of the First World War the 'free' German unions, with a membership of over two million, were the most powerful workers' organizations on the Continent, although they had not yet been able to persuade many large industrialists to accept the principle of collective bargaining. This was not secured until 1918. Although the 'free' unions were closely associated with the Social Democrat Party, they maintained their independence and firmly resisted all attempts by the party to control union policy.

THE CHARTISTS

Political action was another means by which the workers strove to improve their conditions. One of the most striking examples was the Chartist movement in England. In 1836 the London Working Men's Association was established by William Lovett to bring together 'into one bond of unity the intelligent and influential portion of the working class in town and country'. The members were craftsmen and artisans, rather than factory workers. In 1838 the Association prepared a draft Bill for submission to Parliament, which was published as the 'People's Charter'. It contained the famous six points: manhood suffrage, annual parliaments, the secret ballot, the abolition of the property qualification for Members of Parliament, payment of Members of Parliament, and equal electoral districts. The Charter reflected the disappointment of the workers with the Reform Act of 1832, and demanded the establishment of a democratic House of Commons to which working-class candidates would have a real chance of election. It was hoped that the appearance of a powerful workers' party in Parliament would lead to the passing of reforms of benefit to the vast mass of the population.

Although the demands of the Charter were all political in character the movement was inspired by social and economic grievances. As one speaker told a mass meeting on Kersal Moor in Manchester, 'Chartism, my friends, is no mere political movement, where the main point is you getting the

125 *Distribution of the Staves.* Special constables being commissioned on the eve of the Chartist demonstration on Kennington Common, 1848

vote. Chartism is a knife-and-fork question. The Charter means a good house, good food and drink, prosperity and short working hours.' And Ebenezer Elliot declared that Chartism stood for 'free trade, universal peace, freedom of religion, and national education'.

The movement spread from the capital to the industrial districts where it secured the support of many factory workers. In the Midlands it was linked with Thomas Attwood's Birmingham Political Union and in the north the Chartist cause was espoused by such fiery agitators as Feargus O'Connor, Richard Oastler, Julian Harney and J. R. Stephens, who were already attacking the Poor Law and demanding far-reaching factory reforms. O'Connor's *Northern Star* was the leading working-class journal of its day. Great public meetings were held in many parts of the country to elect representatives to a Chartist Convention. This 'People's Parliament' met in London in February 1839 to prepare a petition to accompany the

Charter when it was submitted to Parliament. The debates in the Convention revealed the split between moderate leaders such as Lovett and Attwood, who favoured a policy of peaceful agitation, and extremists such as Feargus O'Connor and Julian Harney, who advocated the violent overthrow of existing institutions. In July the Commons rejected the Charter and several of its leaders were sent to prison. In November John Frost, a member of the Convention, led a band of armed demonstrators to Newport in Monmouthshire to protest against the arrest of Henry Vincent, a popular local Chartist leader. The rising was quickly put down, and Frost was lucky to have his death sentence commuted to transportation.

In the 1840s the movement split into several factions. Those who abhorred violence and believed in constitutional agitation joined either Lovett's new society for the 'political and social improvement of the people' through universal education, or one of the congregations of 'Christian Chartists'. The militants, led by Feargus O'Connor and Bronterre O'Brien, founded the National Charter Association in Manchester in July 1840 and revived a plan for a 'sacred month' during which the country was to be paralysed by a general strike. In the new age of railways and electric telegraphs the government had little difficulty in maintaining law and order. Troops under Sir Charles Napier – who himself appreciated that the workers had genuine grievances for which 'Tory injustice and Whig imbecility' were responsible – overawed the disaffected factory districts.

Despite the dissensions among the Chartists a second Convention, organized by the National Charter Association, was held in London in 1842 and another petition was presented to Parliament. Its rejection was a foregone conclusion. The Plug Plot riots in Lancashire, though not Chartist in origin, gave Chartist extremists a new opportunity to whip up enthusiasm for their cause among the northern factory operatives and miners. Other movements – particularly the well-organized Anti-Corn Law League – appeared to offer the workers more immediate benefits than the Chartists. In 1848, with Europe ablaze with revolutions, the Chartists planned a demonstration on Kennington Common in London to present a third petition to Parliament. The government took vigorous measures to maintain law and order: the Duke of Wellington was responsible for the arrangements and special constables were enrolled to assist the police. Heavy rain, however, dampened the ardour of the demonstrators and the police stopped them from marching on Parliament. The petition reached Westminster in a cab and was found to contain many false signatures. The Chartists, whose threats had alarmed the authorities, now became an object of general derision. The workers returned to industrial action through trade unions in their efforts to secure better pay and conditions, and for many years they made no attempt to influence Parliament by forming a political party of their own. It was not until the 1880s and 1890s that the founding of the Social Democratic Federation, the Fabian Society, and the Independent Labour Party paved the way for a third force in British politics to challenge both the Conservatives and the Liberals.

THE GERMAN SOCIALISTS

In the thirty years during which British workers were improving their condition by founding trade unions, co-operative stores, and friendly societies, German workers were building a powerful socialist party to achieve their aims. In about 1836 a small group of German revolutionary exiles in Paris formed a secret society called 'The League of the Just'. After the failure of Blanqui's rising in 1839, in which its leaders were involved, the League moved to London where its membership was extended so that, instead of being a purely German society, it became international in character. A workers' educational society was formed as a cover for the League's underground activities. In 1843 Friedrich Engels came to London, where he met Karl Schapper, Heinrich Bauer and Josef Moll, some of the League's most active members, and travelled in the north of England, where he came into contact with some of the more militant Chartists, such as Julian Harney. Engels regarded the Chartist movement as the pioneer attempt of the proletariat to play an effective part in politics. In the summer of 1844 Engels visited Karl Marx in Paris and established a friendship which was to have a profound influence upon the development of international socialism. Engels then went home to Barmen, where he completed his book on *The Condition of the Working Class in England*, and became estranged from his father – a highly respectable millowner – by supporting Moses Hess's communist propaganda in the district. In 1845 Marx and Engels met again, in Brussels, where they began their long collaboration as communist writers and agitators. They used the Brussels Correspondence Committee as an organ for the propagation of their views, and in October 1846 Engels reported to the Brussels Committee that he had persuaded a small group of German socialist exiles in Paris to accept his definition of communism. This entailed 'the abolition of private property and its replacement by a community of goods', an objective to be achieved through a 'democratic revolution by force'. Lenin later wrote that the tiny gathering which accepted Engel's definition of communism might be regarded as the seed from which the German socialist party grew.

In the spring of 1847 Moll visited Marx in Brussels and Engels in Paris and invited them to join the League of the Just, at the same time announcing that the League would accept Marx's doctrines and be changed from an underground conspiracy into a public association. Both Marx and Engels accepted, since they felt that a reformed League, with its headquarters in London and branches in Paris and Brussels, would provide an excellent vehicle for their propaganda. In the summer of 1847 the League held its first public conference in London. In Marx's absence – he could not afford the fare from Brussels – Engels expounded his friend's views on the abolition of capitalism and the establishment of a classless society. At the end of November a second conference which both men attended was held in London. A new constitution was approved, the Marxist ideology accepted, and Marx and Engels invited to prepare a public statement concerning the aims of what was now called the 'Communist League'. Engels prepared a brief outline of the League's policy in the form of a catechism, but the *Communist Manifesto* itself was the work of Marx. In the *Manifesto* Marx argued that 'the history of all hitherto existing society is the history of class struggles'. He denounced the evils of the industrial society of his day and foretold the triumph of the workers over their bourgeois oppressors. He criticized earlier forms of socialism – such as those proposed by Robert Owen, Saint-Simon and Weitling – and closed with a ringing challenge to his opponents:

> The communists disdain to conceal their views and aims. They openly declare that their ends can be obtained only by the forcible overthrow of all existing social conditions. Let the ruling classes tremble at a communist revolution. The proletarians have nothing to lose but their chains; they have a world to win. Workers of the world, unite.

126, 127 Friedrich Engels (1820–95) and Karl Marx (1818–83), lifelong friends, champions of the workers and prophets of 'scientific socialism'

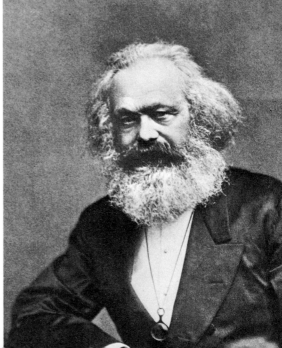

The *Manifesto* was published in London a few days before the fall of the Orléans monarchy in February 1848, but it had little impact upon events in 1848. The few copies that were printed hardly circulated beyond the members of the Communist League in London and their correspondents across the Channel. Marx and a number of his friends went to Cologne where they issued the *Neue Rheinische Zeitung*, which was probably the most widely read revolutionary newspaper of its day. In many European countries the rising of the workers in Paris in June 1848 – ruthlessly put down by General Cavaignac – so alarmed the middle classes that they abandoned their attempts to secure liberal reforms and supported the reaction which restored law and order in one country after another. Schwarzenberg in Austria and Louis Napoleon in France were typical examples of leaders of authoritarian administrations which put down all attempts to introduce parliamentary government and demo-cratic institutions. The trial at Cologne of some of the German communist leaders marked the end of the first phase of the political activities of Marx and Engels. They fled to England, where Marx devoted his time to writing *Das Kapital*, while Engels helped to support him by working for a Manchester cotton firm of which his father was a partner.

It was not until the 1860s that there was a revival of the the working-class movement in Germany. This was the achievement of Ferdinand Lassalle, a leader of the Düsseldorf workers in 1848, previously imprisoned for making inflam-matory speeches. He had visited Marx in London and claimed adherence to the principles of the *Manifesto*. But when he founded the General German Working Men's Association in 1862 he adopted a Chartist, rather than Marxist, programme. A striking success as an orator, he addressed enthusiastic meetings in the industrial Rhineland and demanded, not only universal manhood suffrage, but also the establishment of State-aided co-operative workshops and factories – an echo of Louis Blanc's proposal in France twenty years before. At the height of his brief political career Lassalle's Association probably

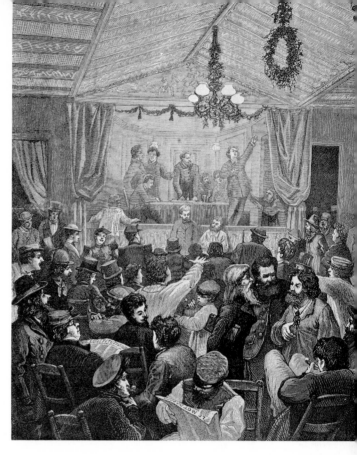

128 A meeting of a Red republican club in Paris, 1871

represented fewer than 5,000 members, but his propaganda tours fired the imagination of the German workers and gave them hope for the future.

Marx and Engels viewed Lassalle's activities with deep suspicion. They regarded him as an opportunist more interested in his own political career than in the welfare of the German workers, and criticized his plans for co-operative factories as a deviation from strict Marxist doctrines. Above all they objected to his entering into private discussions with Bismarck, suspecting him of plotting an unholy alliance with the reactionary forces represented by Prussia's new Minister-President. Lassalle's meteoric career ended dramatically in 1864 when he was killed in a duel. In the same year the International Working

175

Men's Association – the First International – was founded in London and Marx, who soon gained control, was able to use it to propagate his political doctrines.

In the late 1860s the German socialists were split between the Marxist supporters of the First International, led by the elder Wilhelm Liebknecht and August Bebel, and those who accepted the doctrines of Lassalle. A step towards unity was taken in 1869 when the newly formed Social Democrat Party adopted a socialist programme at Eisenach. Six years later the rival factions agreed on the Gotha Programme, which Marx and Engels criticized for making substantial concessions to the followers of Lassalle.

Upon the unification of Germany in 1871 the Reichstag was elected by manhood suffrage and the socialists steadily increased their representation. Initially they were represented by only two members, but in 1877 they polled nearly half a million votes and elected twelve deputies. Bismarck was alarmed at the growth of a party which aimed at the overthrow of the existing order of society, and in 1878, when two attempts were made on the life of the Emperor, took the opportunity to dissolve the Reichstag and hold a general election. The socialist vote declined and the new Reichstag passed a stringent Anti-Socialist Law. The Social Democrat Party was dissolved and its newspapers and periodicals banned. At first its leaders were stunned into submission, but after a conference held at Wyden in Switzerland they accepted Bismarck's challenge and decided to fight him with all the means at their disposal. The party had been driven underground but its propaganda continued. Every week thousands of copies of the *Sozialdemokrat* – published first in Zürich and later in London – were smuggled into Germany. In 1884 the socialists polled nearly 550,000 votes and gained 24 seats in the Reichstag. By 1887 the socialist vote had increased to 763,100. It was clear that the Anti-Socialist Law had completely failed to attain its objective. In 1890, after Bismarck's resignation, the Anti-Socialist Law was allowed to lapse and an attempt to revive it a few years later was frustrated.

129 Some of the many Marxist pamphlets in circulation at about the turn of the century ▶

In 1891 the Social Democrat Party adopted the so-called Erfurt Programme, which did away with the last vestiges of Lassalle's policy. But the breach between Marxists and Lassalleans had scarcely healed when a new controversy broke out among the German socialists. In 1897 Eduard Bernstein suggested that the party should work for the gradual achievement of its aims through peaceful propaganda and reforms rather than through a violent overthrow of the capitalist system. Karl Kautsky vigorously criticized Bernstein's 'revisionism' and appealed to the workers to remain faithful to Marx's doctrines. The supporters of Bernstein gained the day, however, and although the Erfurt Programme remained unchanged, in practice the Social Democrat Party worked only for social reforms to improve the conditions of the workers. Between 1890 and 1914 there were fluctuations in the parliamentary and electoral fortunes of the socialists, but on the eve of the First World War they formed the largest political party in Germany (110 representatives). Yet despite its rapid growth the party had gained no experience in administration, other than at local government level, for none of its leaders was ever appointed to a ministerial post.

THE LUDDITES

When industrial and political action failed it was hardly surprising that the workers in despair turned to violence. The activities of the Luddites and the Plug Plot rioters in England, the Lyons silk-weavers and the syndicalists in France, and the Silesian linen-weavers in Germany brought home to the authorities and public the seriousness of the social problems raised by the Industrial Revolution. Some of these risings were not those of oppressed factory workers, but of craftsmen struggling to survive under adverse economic conditions. They focused attention, however, on the grievances of all sections of the workers.

The Luddite movement in England, which came to a head in 1811–12, began as a rising of the stocking-knitters in the county of Nottingham. At that time the manufacture of hosiery was still a cottage industry. The knitting was done on hand machines in small workshops, but the craftsmen were employed by masters who owned the frames and raw materials. In 1811 the hosiery workers complained that the masters were marketing excessive quantities of fabrics which were both cheap and tawdry. To do this they were cutting wages and inflicting great hardships upon the knitters.

The workers demanded a return to traditional methods of production and previous rates of pay. They were so well organized that it was believed that a single master-mind was planning every move against the manufacturers. It seems probable, however, that several leaders of the machine-breaking bands that terrorized the countryside used the dreaded name of 'General Ludd'. The Luddites operated in groups of about fifty, and descended swiftly upon one village after another, destroying knitting-frames. They disappeared as silently as they had come and the authorities repeatedly failed to catch them. Early in 1812 the Luddite movement spread to the woollen districts of the West Riding and the cotton towns of Lancashire and Cheshire. It was stated in *The Times* on 16 June that a deputation of gentlemen from Lancashire had come to London to inform the government that the Luddites had established several forges in the county in order to manufacture pikes. In Yorkshire the gravest incidents were the midnight assault upon William Cartwright's factory at Liversedge and the murder of the millowner William Horsfall on his way home from Huddersfield market.

It was widely believed that the Luddite attacks on the lives and property of the manufacturers were part of a general plot on the part of the workers to overthrow the government. Robert Southey thought that only the army could save the country from 'an insurrection of the poor against the rich', while Walter Scott declared that 'the country is mined below our feet.' Parliament set up secret committees to inquire into the situation and was informed that the insurgents in the disaffected districts were organized on military lines. Magistrates were given additional powers to cope with the machine-breakers, and in January 1813 seventeen were hanged at York, three for Horsfall's murder and others for the attack on Cartwright's factory. These stern measures helped to restore law and order, though there was a fresh outburst of machine-wrecking in the Midlands in June 1816, when fifty-three frames were destroyed at Heathcote Boden's mill at Loughborough.

WORKERS' RISINGS IN LYONS

Although the industrial growth of France was slower than that of Britain or Germany, the risings of the silk-weavers of Lyons in 1831 and 1834 showed that France too was faced with grave social problems. The manufacture of silks – concentrated in the Lyons district – was one of France's most important industries, producing about 30 per cent of the country's exports. The industry was financed and controlled by some 750 capitalist merchant-manufacturers who had considerable influence on the City Council. Through their agents they distributed the raw materials, collected the finished silks and paid the master-weavers.

There were about 9,000 master-weavers who owned or leased workshops and looms operated by journeymen weavers.

131 Domestic industry was still alive on the Continent late in the nineteenth century: *The Weaver* (*c.* 1883), an etching by Max Liebermann

The weaving-sheds were often small and contained between two and ten hand-looms. The master-weavers were generally responsible for providing accommodation for their workers. Although the master-weavers were small capitalists, many of them operated on so modest a scale that they had much in common with their journeymen. Both groups resented their dependence upon the merchant-manufacturers and felt that they were being exploited by a small group of wealthy and ruthless men. It was hardly surprising that the weavers combined to try to improve their conditions. Trade unions, strikes and picketing were illegal in France, but the weavers of Lyons found a loophole in the law. In 1827 the master-weavers formed what was in effect a trade union under the guise of a friendly society called the *devoir mutuel*. This was a federation of cells each containing twenty men. It was hoped that this method of organizing a union would evade the penalties of the law. In 1831 a mixed commission, consisting of representatives of the *devoir mutuel* and the merchant-manufacturers, drew up a new list of piece-work rates with the assistance of Bouvier du Molart, Prefect of the Rhône Department.

Unfortunately, some manufacturers refused to honour the agreement and this – combined with recent increases in local and national taxation – led the weavers to resort to strike action. That the workers had genuine grievances was shown by a report of the Lyons Chamber of Commerce which condemned a small minority of manufacturers for making large

181

◀ 130 *The Weavers* (*c.* 1895), an etching by Käthe Kollwitz profits at the expense of the workers and recommended the issue of an official list of piece-work rates. A similar proposal came from the official conciliation tribunal (*prud'hommes*), but the refusal of about a hundred manufacturers to pay the new wage rates provoked the workers' rising of November 1831. The insurgents – mainly journeymen weavers from the Croix-Rousse district – gained control of the whole city. By the evening of 22 November General Roquet had withdrawn his troops, leaving the city in the hands of some 30,000 armed insurgents. Some warehouses were set on fire, but the looting of shops was stopped by the workers themselves. Indeed, it was a feature of the rising that law and order was maintained by the insurgents. The revolt ended as suddenly as it had begun. Having made their protest the weavers returned to their homes and the life of the city resumed its normal course. The government sent the Prince of Orléans and Marshal Soult to the scene at the head of over 20,000 soldiers, but their presence was unnecessary. Eleven workers were tried at Riom for their part in the riot – and were acquitted.

The government, however, was still determined to crush the workers of Lyons as soon as a favourable opportunity arose. Marshal Soult announced the annulment of the piece-work rates recently confirmed by the Prefect and the Mayor, and in 1834 the government proposed a new law forbidding the formation of associations even if they had a membership of less than twenty. Since this would make the *devoir mutuel* an illegal organization the silk-weavers of Lyons joined with other workers and with various radical and republican groups, such as the 'Society of the Rights of Man', to resist the proposal. On 5 April there was a disturbance in a law-court when six weavers faced charges in connection with a recent strike. Troops were sent to occupy the hills around the city. When a mob outside the court was dispersed by the soldiers, barricades were erected around half a dozen working-class districts. But within a week the insurrection had been put down and the city was under military rule. Two days later the republicans of

Paris rose in revolt and seized the Rue Transnonian, but were quickly put down by General Bugeaud.

In Germany, the pitiful circumstances of the Silesian hand-loom weavers which culminated in the disturbances of 1844 were largely due to the inability of the German linen industry to adapt itself to machinery and steam. In the eighteenth century German linens had enjoyed a world-wide reputation and exports to South America had earned the currency with which to buy colonial produce such as coffee and sugar. But after the Napoleonic Wars Irish and Belgian machine-woven linens dominated world markets. The Silesian peasants refused to leave the land to work in urban flax-mills. Their earnings dwindled as their masters tried to survive by lowering prices. But reduced prices meant even lower piece-work rates for the workers.

In 1840, shortly after his accession, Fredrick William IV visited Silesia and saw for himself the distress of the weavers. On his instructions Christian von Rother, the Director of the Seehandlung, established a flax-spinning mill at Erdmannsdorf, and soon afterwards co-operated with the merchant August Grossmann in setting up at Wüste Giersdorf the first Prussian wool-textile factory in which power-looms were used. But the Silesian peasant-weavers were still unwilling to leave the land and become full-time factory operatives.

In 1844 there were widespread outbreaks of violence among the weavers, who attacked factories and destroyed machinery. The fury of these German Luddites was also directed against the dwellings of the millowners and managers. The worst riots were at Peterswaldau and Langenbielau. Merckel, the Senior President of the province, had believed in spite of all the evidence, that talk of distress in Silesia had been exaggerated. Now he hurried troops to the scenes of disorder and arrested over eighty rioters. The King sent Minutoli, as a special commissioner, to inquire into the causes of the disorders, and a new attempt was made to tackle the problem by building more factories and roads. Public opinion in Germany was shocked at the revelation of what had driven the Silesian weavers to revolt.

While the workers whose risings have been discussed above were for the most part representatives of a dying industrial system – whose standard of living had been so depressed that outbreaks of violence were almost inevitable – the Plug Plot riots in Lancashire and Cheshire were an example of a rising of factory operatives as distinct from men who plied their crafts in small workshops.

In Britain in 1842 the cotton trade was in the grip of a severe depression: many workers were unemployed or on short time, while the rest were threatened with wage reductions. The scene was set for strikes and riots, and the violent language of some of the advocates of the People's Charter and the repeal of the Corn Laws intensified discontent. In July 1842 an attempt to cut wages at a colliery at Longton led to a strike throughout the north Staffordshire coalfield. The strikers stopped colliery engines by pulling out the boiler plugs and this became a characteristic feature of industrial unrest in Lancashire at this time. The malcontents marched towards Stockport, but were turned back by troops at Poynton.

Soon afterwards several cotton firms in Stalybridge and Ashton-under-Lyne announced wage reductions. On 8 August a Stalybridge mob marched from one mill to another, calling upon the operatives to strike and pulling out boiler plugs to encourage them to do so. The strikers went on to Dukinfield, Ashton, Oldham, Denton and Hyde, visiting cotton-mills and collieries. On 9 August a procession of strikers from Ashton-under-Lyne entered Manchester but was ushered out again by police. At the same time local strikers closed several factories in Manchester. Violence flared up when some millowners locked their gates and refused to be intimidated by the mob. The following day large crowds assembled in Manchester,

132 *Leadenhall Market* (1913) by William Roberts

forced various factories to close, and attacked a gasworks and a police station. The disorders continued, but two days later, with the assistance of 2,500 newly enrolled special constables, the police and the military authorities were able to restore order.

Meanwhile, strikers from Hyde and Ashton-under-Lyne had stopped mills at Glossop, Disley and Stockport, and the workhouse at Stockport was attacked and plundered. Next, the unrest spread south to Macclesfield, Congleton, Leek and the Potteries, and north to many of the Lancashire cotton towns such as Burnley, Bolton, Blackburn, Chorley and Preston. On the whole the authorities had little difficulty in protecting factories, and by the first week of September most of the

185

strikers had drifted back to work. The Manchester power-loom weavers, however, did not give up the struggle until 26 September. Except in a few cases no more was heard of the threatened wage reductions and to that extent the rising achieved its objective.

ANARCHISTS AND SYNDICALISTS

Towards the end of the nineteenth century French extremists such as Sorel, Pouget and Paul Louis attempted to provide an intellectual and philosophical veneer for the doctrine of industrial violence. The activities of the 'syndicalist' section of the French trade-union movement showed how a small fanatical minority of dedicated militants could play a role in industrial politics out of all proportion to the number of their supporters. The rise of the syndicalists in France was closely associated with the anarchist movement, which originated in the latter part of the eighteenth century. William Godwin, whose *Enquiry Concerning Political Justice* appeared in 1793, was one of the earliest anarchists, opposing almost any kind of restraint upon the freedom of the individual. But he advocated the establishment of a new society by peaceful and not by violent methods. Pierre Proudhon, who in 1840 coined the revolutionary slogan 'What is property? Property is theft', also thought that society could be transformed by peaceful means. Yet his view that man was by nature both irrational and violent subsequently had a strong influence upon both left- and right-wing extremists. Mikhail Bakunin, on the other hand, did not merely preach violence, but put his theories into practice. His reputation as a revolutionary was established when he fought at the barricades in Dresden in 1849 and subsequently served a term of imprisonment in Russia and exile in Siberia. He demanded the complete overthrow of 'this effete social world which has become impotent and sterile'. In the 1860s his experience as an agitator in England, Italy and Switzerland convinced him that the down-trodden peasants of Russia, Italy and Spain and the skilled domestic watchmakers of the Swiss Jura were just as ripe for revolution as the industrial proletariat in England. Here he differed from Marx, who believed that revolution must come first in highly industrialized societies.

Bakunin joined the International Working Men's Association and was soon involved in a dispute with Marx which led to the collapse of the Association. While Marx hoped to establish a disciplined political party which would assume authority when existing governments fell, Bakunin denounced communism as 'the negation of liberty' and advocated the establishment of independent communes as the basis for the future organization of society. An anarchist movement, inspired by Bakunin's ideas, flourished in Italy for a time in the 1870s, but Bakunin's greatest success was in Spain. Here his disciple Giuseppe Fanelli established an anarchist movement which remained active until the Civil War of 1936. In the 1880s Prince Kropotkin established his position as the philosopher of the anarchist movement. He had been sent to prison in Russia in 1874 for his revolutionary activities, but escaped and settled in London where he devoted himself to writing and to scientific research.

Early in the twentieth century anarchism appeared to be declining. There were isolated acts of terrorism, but these could hardly be regarded as a serious political movement. Then came a revival of anarchism – particularly in France – when revolutionaries inspired by the views of Bakunin, Kropotkin and Sorel, penetrated the trade-union movement and for a time gained control over it. Taking advantage of widespread social discontent – for not only industrial workers but civil servants, railwaymen, teachers and farm workers also had their grievances – the syndicalists embarked upon a programme of 'direct action', which involved sabotaging machinery, damaging manufactured products, and indulging in go-slow tactics aimed at disrupting the output of factories and the smooth running of transport and postal services. In this way the syndicalists – and their dupes – inflicted the maximum damage upon the public with the minimum of inconvenience

133 *The Pool of London* (1906), by the Fauvist painter André Derain, simultaneously betrays Industrial Man's sense of self-sufficiency and the presence of radical and anarchic currents in the cultural life of Europe

to themselves. It proved to be no easy matter to bring to book men who threw dust into machinery, pulled plugs out of boilers or cut telegraph wires.

The ultimate weapon of the syndicalists was the general strike, which they hoped would bring the existing social order to its knees. In 1899 a Committee of the Confédération Générale du Travail declared that the general strike was 'the only practical method by which the working class can fully liberate itself from the yoke of the capitalists and the government'. By 1906 the propaganda of the syndicalists had become so active and so violent that the authorities feared that the May-Day demonstrations would lead to a rising of the workers in Paris. In March and in May 1909 there were national strikes of postal and telegraph workers. In October 1910 a strike on the Northern Railway spread to other lines, and Briand, the Prime Minister, who was himself a socialist, called up the reservists. Many strikers were conscripted in this way and had to do in uniform the work they had refused to do in civilian dress. By 1914 firm action by successive governments had coped with the menace of syndicalism, and the French people had made it clear that they would not be held to ransom by a handful of fanatics.

In Spain there had been an anarchist movement inspired by Bakunin's ideas since the 1870s. It appealed to the industrial workers of Barcelona and Bilbao, the coal-miners of the Asturias and the smallholders and landless farm workers of southern Spain. The insurrection of the paper workers of Alcoy in 1873, when factories were burned down and the Mayor was killed, showed that the introduction of modern industries into Spain had been accompanied by social problems with which older manufacturing countries had long been familiar. In the 1880s and 1890s the anarchists promoted industrial strife and peasant risings. In 1911 the Confederación Nacional de Trabajo was founded and, like the French federation of trade unions on which it was modelled, was dominated by anarchists. Meanwhile, anarchist doctrines made headway among the peasants, particularly in Andalusia, where rural conditions were exceptionally bad.

Anarchism spread from Europe to North and South America. The expanding manufacturing regions of the United States, where the social evils associated with early industrialization were as serious as they had been in Europe, proved to be a fertile field for the activities of the anarchists. In Chicago in 1886, for example, anarchists exploited the grievances of strikers at the McCormick harvester works, and there were serious riots involving loss of life. In Central and South America, Italian and Spanish anarchists took full advantage of the discontent among oppressed peasants, miners and industrial workers.

On the eve of the First World War anarchists and syndicalists appeared to be challenging Socialists for the leadership of the working-class movement. Beatrice Webb wrote in 1912: 'Syndicalism has taken the place of the old-fashioned Marxism. The angry youth, with bad complexion, frowning brow and weedy figure is nowadays a syndicalist; the glib young workman whose tongue runs away with him today mouths the phrases of French syndicalism instead of those of German social democracy.'

EMIGRATION

If all else failed, one safety-valve remained. This was emigration. Between 30 and 35 million people left Europe in the nineteenth century to settle overseas. The numbers emigrating rose from about 310,000 in the 1820s to 2,500,000 in the 1840s and over 7,000,000 in the 1880s. In the first half of the nineteenth century the United Kingdom and Germany supplied the majority of the emigrants. Most of the migrants from western Europe sought new homes in the United States and in British colonies suitable for white settlement, but some emigrants from Central Europe moved eastwards, and between 1800 and 1830 some 130,000 immigrants settled in Russia. The fact that emigration increased after a trade depression suggests that the decision to

134 *The Arrival* (1914), by Christopher Nevinson, announces the climax
of the Age of Progress and the dawn of the industrial Millennium

135 The Departure. An emigrant couple gaze wistfully over the stern-rails in *The Last of England* (1864–6) by Ford Madox Brown

settle in a new country was strongly influenced by a determination to escape from unemployment, poverty or even starvation. All types of workers emigrated: Irish peasants, Scottish crofters, English hand-loom weavers, smallholders from south-west Germany, as well as craftsmen and factory operatives from the industrial regions. In the early nineteenth century the hardships and dangers of the Atlantic crossing in 'coffin ships' operated by unscrupulous owners made emigration a hazardous undertaking, but the coming of the iron steamship and the improved organization of emigration facilities at ports like Liverpool and Bremen enabled those leaving Europe to do so in greater safety and comfort. Earlier in the industrial age governments and employers generally regarded workers – particularly skilled artisans – as a national asset to be kept at home. In France the emigration of qualified craftsmen had been forbidden since

193

136, 137 Below, the incentive to emigrate, a cartoon of 1849. Right, *Meal Time*: between-decks on an emigrant ship, 1872

Colbert's Edict of 1669. In England earlier enactments to prevent artisans from leaving the country were consolidated in an Act of 1794 and it was not until 1825 that this Act was repealed. It may be doubted, however, whether such attempts to restrict emigration were very successful.

EUROPE IN 1914

By 1914 the condition of the workers in the more advanced manufacturing districts was very different from what it had been during the initial phase of the Industrial Revolution. Their standard of living had improved considerably. The worst conditions were now to be found, not in highly industrialized countries like Britain or Germany, but in newly industrialized countries like Russia and in underdeveloped regions, such as

138
A Russian emigrant
family in the early
twentieth century
immediately after
disembarking at
New York

Spain, where the machine age was only in its infancy. In the major industrial countries of western Europe the worst abuses of industrialization were disappearing. This was due partly to the efforts of the workers themselves, partly to the efforts of governments and local authorities, and partly to the work of humanitarian reformers and the more enlightened employers. Since children now had to go to school they could no longer work in factories. Women had disappeared from the mines. Men had achieved shorter working hours either by agreement with their employers or by legislative enactment. Factories and mines were safer, though occupational diseases had not been eliminated and colliery disasters reminded the public from time to time of the hazards still faced by those who produced the coal so essential to the life of an industrial community.

The environment of the workers had also improved. Some slum property had disappeared when city-planners had begun to rebuild old centres of industry. Disgusting cesspools and streams that served as open sewers were largely things of the past. Pure water and adequate sanitation were now the rule rather than the exception. The preservation of open spaces – Epping Forest, the Bois du Boulogne, the Tiergarten – gave workers and their families a chance to escape occasionally from smoky overcrowded cities into the open air. As compared with the early nineteenth century the industrial workers now lived longer, consumed a more varied diet, wore better clothes and enjoyed better health.

The workers had also achieved some success in curbing the power of their masters. Employers were no longer free to do exactly what they pleased in their mines and factories. They had to accept shorter hours, safer working conditions, and the payment of wages in cash. In some industries they were faced with powerful trade unions, which were constantly pressing for better terms of employment for their members.

As a citizen, too, the position of the workers in advanced industrial countries had improved. The workers had the vote and had organized their own political parties. In France a

139 The rise of a popular culture and of a working class
with time for leisure and money for recreation,
reflected in *The Cardiff Team* (1912–13), by Robert Delaunay ▶

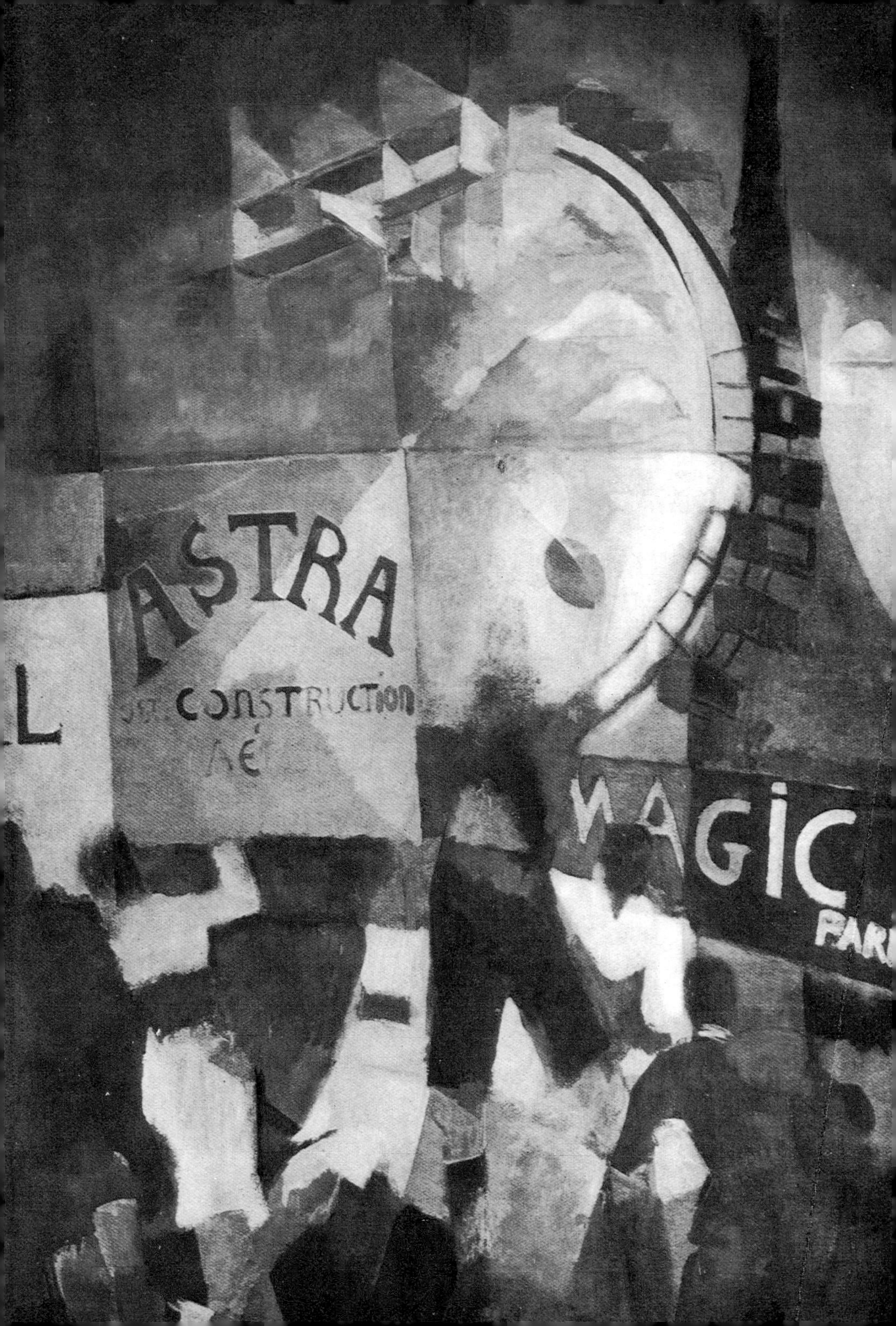
ASTRA
CONSTRUCTION
MAGIC

140 Symbols of achievement, a balloon, a dirigible and a biplane yet seem to brood over this scene, *View of the Pont de Sèvres* (1908) by Rousseau

socialist had held office as Prime Minister and in Germany the Social Democrat Party was the largest in the Reichstag. At local government level the representatives of the workers sat on municipal councils, school-boards and Poor Law committees, and made their influence felt in the day-to-day administration of the towns in which they lived.

Karl Marx had argued that under capitalism the rich would inevitably become richer and the poor poorer. Events showed that he had been mistaken. The more hard-working and thrifty workers were not sinking into deeper poverty but were themselves becoming capitalists in a modest way. They put money into savings banks, friendly societies, building societies and co-operative societies.

141 Part of the first design for a city to follow out the implications of the Industrial Revolution. Devised by Tony Garnier, 1899–1904 ▶

The social evils brought about by industrialization, however, had only been partially eradicated. If the condition of some workers had improved, that of others had not. There were casual workers and unskilled men who earned very low wages and enjoyed no security of employment. The continued survival of a pool of labour – a 'reserve army' of unemployed – showed that at least one of the major problems of industrialization had proved to be singularly intractable. And the economy appeared to be as unstable as ever. Man had triumphed over cholera and typhus, but had not mastered the financial crisis or the trade depression. The possibility of capitalist planning – of controlling economic fluctuations – still lay in the future.

ORIGINS OF THE INDUSTRIAL REVOLUTION

Ashton, T. S.
The Industrial Revolution 1760–1930 (1948)
An Economic History of England: the Eighteenth Century (1955). A particularly useful survey by the leading English authority on the Industrial Revolution in Britain

Beales, H. L.
The Industrial Revolution (2nd edn. 1958)

Clapham, J. H.
Economic Development of France and Germany (new edn. 1961)

Clough, S. B.
France. A History of National Economics 1789–1939 (1939)
The Economic History of Modern Italy (1964)

Court, H. W. B.
A Concise Economic History of Britain from 1750 to Recent Times (1954)

Dunham, A. L.
The Industrial Revolution in France (1953)

Flinn, M. W.
The Origins of the Industrial Revolution (1966)
An Economic and Social History of Britain 1066–1939 (1961). An excellent introductory survey

Hammond, J. L. and Barbara
The Rise of Modern Industry (5th edn. 1937)

Hayek, F. A.
Capitalism and the Historians (1954)

Henderson, W. O.
The Industrial Revolution on the Continent (1961)
The Zollverein (2nd edn. 1959)

Hill, Christopher
Reformation to Industrial Revolution (1967)

Hobsbawn, E. J.
The Age of Revolution 1789–1848 (1962; Mentor Book, 1964). An analysis of the effects upon the world of the French Revolution and the Industrial Revolution

Hobson, J. A.
The Evolution of Modern Capitalism (1894; new edn. 1926)

Hoffmann, W. G.
The Growth of Industrial Economies (translated by W. O. Henderson and W. H. Chaloner, 1958)

Landes, D. S. (ed.)
The Rise of Capitalism (1964)

Lenin, N.
The Development of Capitalism in Russia (1899; English translation, Moscow, 1956)

List, Friedrich
The National System of Political Economy (1841; new edn. 1966)

Mantoux, P.
The Industrial Revolution of the Eighteenth Century in England (revised edn. 1961)

Mavor, J.
An Economic History of Russia (2nd edn., 2 vols, 1925)

Nef, J.
The Conquest of the Material World (1964)

Nussbaum, F.L.	*A History of the Economic Institutions of Modern Europe* (1935). This is a summary of Werner Sombart, *Der moderne Kapitalismus* (4th edn., 3 vols, 1921–8), an important standard work
Redford, Arthur	*The Economic History of England 1760–1860* (1936)
Rostow, W.W.	*The Process of Economic Growth* (1952)
	The Stages of Economic Growth (1960)
Sombart, Werner	*The Jews and Modern Capitalism* (1913)
Stolper, G.	*German Economy 1870–1940* (1940)
Veblen, T.	*Imperial Germany and the Industrial Revolution* (1939)
Weber, A.	*Growth of Cities in the Nineteenth Century* (1899)

THE INVENTORS

Bernal, J.D.	*Science and Industry in the Nineteenth Century* (1953)
Chaloner, W.H. and Musson, A.E.	*Industry and Technology* (1963)
Dickinson, H.W.	*A Short History of the Steam Engine* (new edn. 1963)
Hatfield, H.S.	*The Inventor and his World*
Hughes, T.P. (ed.)	*The Development of Western Technology since 1500* (1964)
Jewkes, Sawers and Stillerman	*The Sources of Invention* (new edn. 1961)
McCloy, S.T.	*French Inventions of the Eighteenth Century* (1952)
Matschoss, Conrad	*Great Engineers* (1938)
Singer, C. (*et al.*)	*A History of Technology, Vol. IV The Industrial Revolution* (1958)
Usher, A.P.	*A History of Mechanical Inventions* (revised edn. 1954)
Wilson, G.B.L.	'The Evolution of Technology' (in G.S.Métraux and F.Crouzet, *The Nineteenth Century World*, 1963)
Wolf, A.	*A History of Science, Technology and Philosophy in the 16th and 17th Centuries* (1935)
	A History of Science, Technology and Philosophy in the 18th Century (1938)
Zvorikine, A.A.	'Inventions and Scientific Ideas in Russia' (in G.S. Métraux and F.Crouzet, *The Nineteenth Century World*, 1963)

THE ENTREPRENEURS

Berdrow, W.	*The Letters of Alfred Krupp* (1930)
Crump, W.B. (ed.)	*The Leeds Woollen Industry 1780–1820* (1931)
Filton, R.S. and Wadsworth, A.P.	*The Strutts and the Arkwrights 1758–1830* (1958)
Henderson, W.O.	*The State and the Industrial Revolution in Prussia 1740–1870* (1958)
	Britain and Industrial Europe (2nd edn. 1965)
	J.C. Fischer, his Diary of Industrial England 1814–51 (1966)
	Industrial Britain under the Regency (1968)

Klass, G. von	*Krupps: the Story of an Industrial Empire* (1954)
Laue, T.H. von	*Sergei Witte and the Industrialization of Russia* (1963)
Lyashchenko, P.T.	*History of the National Economy of Russia* (1949)
Menne, B.	*Krupp, or the Lords of Essen* (1937)
Pollard, S.	*The Genesis of Modern Management* (1965)
Rimmer, W G.	*Marshalls of Leeds. 1788–1886* (1960)
Rosovsky, H.	'The Serf Entrepreneur in Russia' (*Explorations in Entrepreneurial History*, Vol. VI, No. 4, 1953–4)
Siemens, Werner von	*Inventor and Entrepreneur: Recollections of Werner von Siemens* (1966). First English edition was published as *Personal Recollections of Werner von Siemens*)
Smiles, Samuel	*Lives of the Engineers* (3 vols. 1861–2)
	Industrial Biography: Ironworkers and Toolmakers (1863)
Sombart, Werner	*The Jews and Modern Capitalism* (1913)
Urwin, G. (*et al.*)	*Samuel Oldknow and the Arkwrights* (1924)
Witte, Sergei	*The Memoirs of Count Witte* (1921)

THE WORKERS

Ashley, W.J.	*The Progress of the German Working Classes in the Last Quarter of a Century* (1904)
Briggs, Asa (ed.)	*Chartist Studies* (1959)
Buer, M.C.	*Health, Wealth and Population in the Early Days of the Industrial Revolution* (1926)
Carrothers, W.A.	*Emigration from the British Isles* (1929)
Carr-Saunders, A.M. (*et al.*)	*Consumers' Co-operation in Great Britain* (1938)
Cole, G.D.H.	*Chartist Portraits* (1941)
	A Century of Co-operation (1945)
Dawson, W.H.	*Social Insurance in Germany 1883–1911* (1912)
Engels, Friedrich	*The Condition of the Working Class in England* (1845, English translation by W.O.Henderson and W.H. Chaloner, 1958)
	Selected Writings (Penguin, 1967, ed. by W.O.Henderson)
Fay, C.R.	*Co-operation at Home and Abroad* (1908)
	Life and Labour in the Nineteenth Century (1920)
Gaskell, Peter	*The Manufacturing Population of England* (1833)
Hammond, J.L. and Barbara	*The Village Labourers 1760–1832* (1911)
	The Rise of Modern Industry (5th edn. 1937)
Hovell, M.	*The Chartist Movement* (1918; new edn. 1950)
Jellinek, F.	*The Paris Commune of 1871* (1937)
Joll, J.	*The Anarchists* (1964)
Kuczynski, Jürgen	*Labour Conditions in Western Europe 1820 to 1935* (1937)
Levine, L.	*Syndicalism in France* (1914)
McKay, D.C.	*The National Workshops* (1933)

Marx, Karl	*Capital*, Vol. I, 1867 (translated by E. and G. Paul, 1928)
Mehring, Franz	*Karl Marx. The Story of his Life* (translated by E. Fitz-gerald, 1936)
Montgomery, B. G.	*British and Continental Labour Policy* (1922)
Orth, S. P.	*Socialism and Democracy in Europe* (1913)
Russell, Bertrand	*German Social Democracy* (1896)
Saunders, W. S.	*Trade Unionism in Germany* (1916)
Sombart, Werner	*Socialism and the Social Movement* (1896, English translation 1909)
Webb, S. and B.	*History of Trade Unionism* (1893; revised edn. 1920)
	English Local Government: English Poor Law History Part I (1927), Part II (2 vols, 1929)

LIST OF ILLUSTRATIONS

205

208

INDEX

Numbers in italics refer to illustrations

The author wishes to thank Dr W. H. Chaloner for reading the proofs.